PRAISE FOR

Schwartz's Hebrew Delicatessen: The Story

"Breezy, humorous prose... a taut narrative full of
eye-openers and local legend... a welcome addition to
Montreal lore and a good, old-fashioned read."
—Montreal Gazette

"A frequently fascinating, always entertaining examination
of one of the last unexplored corners of Montreal urban
folklore, told with wit and exuberance, and must-read
material for all Montrealers."
—Hour Magazine

"Bill Brownstein offers us a delicious history of this
Montreal landmark with its secret recipe, eccentric owners,
and clients of all nationalities, from Montreal
and around the world."
—La Presse

"An incredibly well-researched chronicle that reads like a
collection of short stories."
—Maisonneuve Magazine

The author behind the counter.

Bill Brownstein

Véhicule Press

Published with the generous assistance of the Canada Book Fund of
the Department of Canadian Heritage and the Société de
développement des entreprises culturelles du Québec (SODEC).

Cover art and design: Michel Rabagliati
Set in Adobe Minion by Simon Garamond
Printed by Marquis Book Printing Inc.

LIBRARY AND ARCHIVES CANADA CATALOGUING IN PUBLICATION

Schwartz's Hebrew delicatessan : the story
Bill Brownstein

ISBN 1-55065-296-3

1. Schwartz's Montreal Hebrew Delicatessen–History.
2. Smoked meat–Québec (Province)–Montréal–History.
I. Title.

TX945.5.S38B76 2010   647.95714'28   C2011-905338-9

Published by Véhicule Press, Montréal, Québec, Canada
www.vehiculepress.com

Distribution in Canada by LitDistCo
orders@litdistco.ca

Distribution in U.S. by Independent Publishers Group
www.ipgbook.com

Printed and bound in Canada.

In memory of my father, who brought me into this deli demimonde.

Acknowledgements

Jack Lieber; Liz Ferguson; Hy Diamond, Frank Silva, Mike Nelli and the rest of the Schwartz's gang of waiters, cutters, dishwashers and gossips; Morris "The Shadow" Sherman; Ryan Larkin; William Weintraub; Simon Dardick and Nancy Marrelli of Véhicule Press; and, of course, Debi or Deb, who actually learned to love karnatzel.

Contents

True Story

John Zorn is not a demanding man. The veteran alto sax blower
is a frequent performer at the Montreal International Jazz Festival.
He's not one of those kooks who insist that the orange M&Ms be
separated from the rest of the batch and placed in a silver bowl in
his dressing room. Nah. But the jazzbo is particularly cranky about
one thing in Montreal: smoked meat. In his contract rider a few
years back, he simply requested Schwartz's smoked meat for a nosh
prior to showtime. Instead, he was sent smoked meat from a lesser
dispenser downtown—one of those faux delis who would dare to
meld smoked meat and pizza and, yech, spaghetti in one dish.
Zorn was not amused. In a fit of carnivorous rage, he chucked the
bogus smoked meat against the wall of his hotel room.

And he refused to perform until he was given the real deli
deal. His show was held up nearly half an hour. His fans were
growing restless. But jazz-fest founder André Ménard finally saved
the day by rushing out to the deli himself and delivering sandwiches
from Schwartz's. He also defended Zorn's actions. "I demand the
best in music for my festival," Ménard explained. "And he demands
the best in smoked meat. Life may be full of compromises, but not
when it comes to smoked meat. John was perfectly right to be picky.
I am, too. Schwartz's is king. There is no substitute."

Introduction

IT WAS A GREY AUTUMN DAY in 1955. There was a chill in the air. Many were preoccupied with the Cold War, with fears that the Soviets could trigger nuclear Armageddon and that North Americans would soon be kissing their butts goodbye. And yet these were, oddly enough, golden days for this naive kindergarden student.

Montreal, according to my wizened elders, was bustling with activity. The buzz was that the night life in the city was second to none. Sin City, as it was often referred to and romanticized back then, was attracting big-name hoofers like Sammy Davis Jr. and big-name strippers like Lili St. Cyr. Bars stayed open all night. Illicit gambling parlours and brothels flourished. Montreal was the financial power centre of Canada back then—or so we were led to believe. Hell, Toronto closed up for the night around 9 p.m.

Montreal was also a football power in that era. In the Canadian Football League, anyway. Led by quarterback Sam "The Rifle" Etcheverry and his favourite receiver, "Prince" Hal Patterson, the Montreal Alouettes made it to the Grey Cup the year before, only to be stymied by those cursed Edmonton Eskimos. But this was another season, and again the Als were poised to go all the way. And, best of all, it was deigned by the power that be, my father, that I was old enough to attend, with him, my very first Als football game at Percival Molson Stadium, to be surrounded by flask-toting fans in raccoon coats, forever screaming at the refs: "There are three kinds of robins: the red robin, the blue robin—and, you, ya robbin' bastard." A true rite *de passage.*

Of course, there was a ritual to be followed on game day. Before parking our cheeks on those cold, splinter-rich seats of Molson Stadium, a visit to Schwartz's Deli on the Main was *de rigueur.* This was to be my first visit and, thus, to be part of my official ascent into manhood. I was about to become indoctrinated into a cult—albeit one which would require a thorough shower after every visit.

Even back then, Schwartz's had almost a mythical quality. It was Montreal's melting pot. It lay smack in the centre of the city's Mason-Dixon Line, on St. Laurent Boulevard, bridging east and west. It was there that sidewalk philosophers, cabbies, hookers, bookies, visiting celebs, garmentologists, dermatologists, dentists, college students and politicos, of all cultural backgrounds and economic strata, would converge to chew the fat, literally.

So, it was with a mix of considerable excitement and trepidation that I entered the demimonde of Schwartz's that fateful autumn day. I didn't know what to expect, but for all the hype surrounding the place, I think I expected more than your garden-variety dive with curt—with gusts to rude—waiters who would just as soon you never graced them with your presence. Decor was decidedly non-existent—an homage to broken tiles, linoleum and arborite at best. Seats at the counter looked like they might give at any second. Tables looked equally shaky. The place was thick with smoke and steam—only some of which emanated from the dozens of briskets behind the counter and in the window. And oversized people abounded, for these were the days before most humans counted calories. And yet this ramshackle place was a piece of paradise at the same time. It was like a twisted sort of mini-United Nations, with everyone trying to out-holler the next person in English, French, Italian, Greek, Yiddish, German, Romanian, Portuguese, Chinese and, in my case, Pig-Latin.

My father, a no-nonsense kind of guy who spent an inordinate amount of time toiling in the shmata trade nearby, appeared in his element. He was loose, laughing and shmoozing with buddies from the 'hood. He was born a couple of blocks away and grew up in the area. My mother was actually born upstairs from the famed Warshaw's grocery store, a stone's throw from Schwartz's.

The Main had more than its share of delis, but Schwartz's— or the Montreal Hebrew Delicatessen or the Charcuterie Hébraïque de Montréal as it is almost never referred to by either anglophone or francophone worshippers—was the place to see and to be seen. It was, with apologies to Brother André and the St. Joseph's Oratory and, for that matter, the Forum, the home of the Montreal Canadiens, hockey's answer to the New York Yankees, a veritable shrine. And, honestly, Schwartz's mouth-watering medium-fat smoked meat sandwiches were about as heavenly a treat one could cram into the mouth.

Word was that founder Reuben Schwartz had a recipe for smoked meat more closely guarded than the vault to Fort Knox. Sure, Schwartz's served dynamite rib steaks, smoked turkey and goose, salami, karnatzels and, lest we forget, spek. Ah, spek, a mound of pure, unadulterated, artery-clogging fat, trimmed from the brisket, and topped with an array of heartburn-inducing spices. Spek, as the regular garmentologists would muse, was probably responsible for killing more Jews than those Nazi bastards.

But it was the smoked meat and, of course, the characters that were the draws at Schwartz's. If you wanted to know what was happening in the city, Schwartz's was the barometer. Smoked meat was the conduit. It was, and still is, the beef that binds Montreal.

Can't even recall who won the football game that grey autumn afternoon in 1955. But I will never forget the first of fifty years' worth of pilgrimages to Schwartz's. And, of course, the subsequent gas. Everything has its price.

One

It's Been a Long, Strange Trip

IT'S A QUESTION that has apparently baffled even the Talmudic scholars: Who invented smoked meat? There was no shortage of folks willing to take credit. In fact, scores of Romanian-born Jews who immigrated to Montreal at the turn of the twentieth century had insisted they brought this time-honoured recipe for pickling and smoking with them to the New World.

I must come clean here. For a few heady years in my youth, I laboured under the illusion that a great-great grandfather was the man behind the meat. A relative confided to me that this supposed inventor had also been the court jester to the royal court of Romania, before getting a little too cocky with the king—evidently, the old seltzer-spraying boutonniere gag hastened his sacking—and being forced to flee the kingdom with only his smoked-meat recipe and his family. He managed to elude sabre-wielding Cossacks on horseback—or the Romanian facsimile—and emerge on Montreal's Main with tales to tell and salamis to sell.

Alas, the story turned out to be fantasy. No, not the part about being court jester to the king. He was. (And evidently I was named after him. The plot thickens.) Seems that it was, actually, a great-great grandfather on my mother's side—not the kibbitzer on my father's side—who was the smoked-meat pioneer. A veritable Samuel de Champlain of spice.

According to a great aunt, this great-great grandfather, Itzak Rudman, arrived in Montreal with his wife Malka in 1902, following turbulent stints in Turkey, Egypt and Romania, whose

BILL BROWNSTEIN

inhabitants clearly didn't appreciate quality spek. My great-great grandfather settled into an apartment a few blocks away from what would be the location of Schwartz's some twenty-six years later. Though a man of modest means, not given to over-achieving on the commerce front, Rudman was known as an accomplished "voorstmaker," a creator of smoked meat and salami. His schmaltz—pure unadulterated chicken fat that could trigger a coronary mere moments after being ingested—was second to none. His children helped him grind up the ingredients—don't ask—in a back room of his crammed Cadieux Street (later de Bullion Street) flat. Folks came from all over the area to buy and savour his meats.

Evidently, one merely had to follow the scent of garlic to find his spot on the corner of Cadieux and Duluth. According to family lore, Rudman, who passed away in 1928 at the age of 72, taught Max Lester, of Lester's deli fame, the fine art of mak-ing smoked meat. Of course, according to Lester family lore, Max claimed to have brought the recipe for smoked meat to Montreal himself in 1925. So it went in the deli trenches.

Not to detract from my great-great grandfather's pickling prowess or that of Max Lester, but they were hardly the only ones in the 'hood responsible for the digestive-tract problems relating to the consumption of deli. There were many others renowned for their meat-smoking feats. And virtually all had something in common. They were Romanian Jews—like Schwartz's credited founder Reuben Schwartz. And like my great-great grandfather, they were gypsies of a sort, too. Prior to settling in—and then splitting—Romania, they, too, spent time in Turkey and Egypt. It wasn't a matter of not appreciating the weather that caused them to move so often. It was more a matter of not always being appreciated by the ruling classes.

Smoked goose pastrami started appearing, not-so-

16

coincidentally with the arrival of Romanian immigrants on this side of the Atlantic, mainly in New York City and Montreal, toward the end of the nineteenth century. But the goose was soon cooked—metaphorically speaking. North Americans weren't much fussy about this form of fowl. Plus, the beef industry began to really flourish. As a consequence, butchers replaced the goose with brisket, a cut of beef taken from the breast and lower chest sections. The brisket was also referred to as the peasant cut, because of the fat and sinew content, not to mention the bargain-basement price back then.

And thus pastrami was born in North America. In Montreal, though, it was and has always been referred to as smoked meat, which can be differentiated from pastrami or corned beef by its higher ratio of fat and spice, which connoisseurs will attest accounts for its superior taste.

The word pastrami actually comes from the Turkish "basturma," which only sounds like a profanity relating to an offspring without a known father. Basturma was sliced meat, which was wind-dried, pickled with dry spices, then pressed together again. Turkish soldiers were issued basturma as army rations, and the belief was that if the troops couldn't blow the enemy off the battlefield with their military strategy, they could at least blow them off with their breath. Evidently, the Turks cured their meat with an inordinate amount of garlic, black pepper and paprika. And so the recipe was passed down to Romanian peddlers, who brought it over with them to North America and who came up with the idea of sandwiching the delicacy, served steaming hot or cold, between slices of rye bread and complementing the meal with coleslaw, sour pickles and tomatoes and peppers. A half-century later, French fries and a libation—cherry Coke or black cherry soda—were added to round out the perfect deli repast.

But before that, stories persisted about thirteenth-century French Jews who were mocked because they perceived God only when chowing down on beef pickled with vinegar and garlic. Evidently, this combo could elicit a euphoria—not unlike that experienced by a Schwartz's devotee. There were also reports that Italian Jews in the sixteenth century subsisted on smoked goose, duck and meat, dried, cured and pressed in a similar manner to the style of the Turks.

No question, however, that pastrami was perfected by Romanian immigrants to New York City, and it was their off-spring who opened, and who continue to operate, such deli landmarks as the Carnegie, the Stage and Katz's. Such is the popularity of pastrami in the Big Apple that the Pastrami Olympics was held there in 1973 to determine the best in the city.

No such Smoked Meat Olympics has yet to be held in Montreal. But over the years, in polls conducted by newspapers and in panels of critics, Schwartz's, founded by Romanian immigrant Reuben Schwartz in 1928, is invariably the smoked meat of choice. Not that there hasn't been serious competition. Montreal is top-heavy with delis that go back to the early days of Schwartz's. Not far from Schwartz's, there was Benny's, not to be confused with the downtown Ben's, and Kravitz's, from the family that spawned Ben's. As for Ben's, it was started in 1908 by another branch of the Kravitz clan who had immigrated from Lithuania. While smoked meat was its mainstay, Ben's, which met its demise in 2007, became more of all-purpose restaurant-delicatessen.

Then there was the Ben Ash chain, and when one of the outlets was sold, the owner had the brainwave of cutting outdoor sign costs by switching the name to Den Ash. Lester's, Snowdon Deli and the Main, across the street from Schwartz's, have been around for eons and have more than their share of boosters, as did the Brown Derby before closing its doors and broiler. In the outer reaches of the city, there is Chenoy's, Smoked Meat Pete and Abie's—the latter founded by a former Schwartz's employee.

So what separates Schwartz's from the rest of the smoked-meat pack? For starters, Schwartz's, unlike most of the others, doesn't use artificial preservatives. Schwartz's also takes its sweet —actually, spicey—time, which is mandatory because the beef can be so tough. Schwartz's prepares its smoked meat in a traditional way with a secret mixture of herbs and spices, and marinates it for between ten to fourteen days in barrels, before spending a working day in Reuben Schwartz's original smoker adjacent to the kitchen, in the back of the restaurant. To feed the masses, thousands of pounds of brisket are purchased every week, usually from Alberta.

Ironically, smoked meat was created largely as a means to preserve meat from rotting in an age that had yet to develop modern refrigeration methods. Although this technique for curing and preserving is no longer necessary today, the flavour of the smoked meat has proved to be such a hit that no one is prepared to bid adieu to the process. Thus, the Schwartz's legend persists.

Advertisement, in Yiddish, for the newly-opened
"kosher-style" Montreal Hebrew Delicatessan, 1928.

Two

May the Schwartz Be with You

THE PUFF OF SMOKE finally came. It was April 1, 2004, but this was no joking matter. After some intense deliberation, it had been deemed by the deli gods and a conclave of fresser cardinals that there would be but one Schwartz's, to be situated on the Main where founder Reuben Schwartz first started smoking his meats back in 1928.

Schwartz's latest ruler, the avuncular Hy Diamond, had long been mulling over plans to open a second deli in downtown Montreal. Diamond had been bombarded with offers from far and wide to franchise. Some were offering pots of gold. Diamond was distressed. Hard to say no to pots of gold, yet harder still to break with a seventy-six-year tradition. What would customers say?

Diamond describes himself as a mere mortal caretaker, placed on this planet to ensure no harm will ever come to the Schwartz name. The deli, he acknowledges, is much bigger than him. Word of its popularity has spread to every corner of the planet. The dozens of accolades adorning the walls of Schwartz's say it all: "A Beef on Rye to Freeze to Death for!" London's *Financial Times*; "Schwartz's is the best smoked meat in Montreal, and therefore in the world!" *Gourmet*; "The best place in the Milky Way to sample smoked-meat sandwiches!" *Time* magazine; "When you're in Montreal, you must go to Schwartz's." *The New York Times*; "A Montreal legend for 75 years. So what's the big deal? It's the *viande fumée* that overwhelms two slices of rye." *National Geographic*.

Yet it would have been almost every downtown-dwelling deli lover's dream—a Schwartz's old-fashioned smoked-meat sandwich to devour hot and be savoured on their home turf — without having to schlep over to the Main to pick it up. In what could have been one of the more earth-shattering eating developments in recent years, Diamond had been considering plans to set up this second deli on a prime Crescent Street location between de Maisonneuve Boulevard and Ste. Catherine Street.

Besides the cross atop Mount Royal, there is probably no more identifiable Montreal trademark than Schwartz's, which has been churning out smoked-meat sandwiches and other deli delights on St. Laurent Boulevard since Reuben Schwartz opened shop here on New Year's Eve, 1928, just prior to the Great Depression. Talk about timing. Diamond and Schwartz's manager Frank Silva then had to deal with a dilemma that could easily trigger depression among staff and customers, among all Montrealers: Should there be only one Schwartz's? Would Montrealers accept a downtown franchise?

This was not the first time the Schwartz team has been asked to consider setting up a second operation. Offers have come to open in other downtown locations, Montreal's West Island, the Laurentians and even Toronto. But what would have made the move to Crescent more tempting is that, like the Main, this is a street that never sleeps.

One didn't have to be an economist to come to the conclusion a Schwartz's on Crescent would clean up. Frankly, there is no other deli in the area that comes close to it. Plus, the place would feed off workers downtown for lunch and dinner, night owls in the wee hours and tourists all the time. And, best of all for management, such a move probably wouldn't cut into the business on the Main.

Still, Diamond and Silva weren't quite convinced. "I was

down in New York recently and went to Katz's deli, which has been around for 118 years," said Diamond "There is only one Katz. There is only one Carnegie Hall. And there has only been one Schwartz here. It's unique. People sometimes line up for hours to get in."

Added Silva: "They always say everything in this city is changing. Except Schwartz's. It is an institution in Montreal and perfection can be hard to duplicate."

Yet Diamond and Silva didn't deny the many advantages to having a second Schwartz's. The locations Diamond was eyeing would be much larger, able to accommodate far more customers than the 61 that can be served at a time on the Main, as well as a smoking and marinating facility for the meat. And who knew? Maybe some booze to go down with the chow and the shmooze. Schwartz's on the Main has never had a liquor license. And dare we say, dessert! Schwartz's has always eschewed dessert. No, silly, not because management was ever concerned by customers taking on excess cake-age calories. Rather, dessert meant coffee and chat and lingering. The name of the game in deli is turn-over, and few on the planet turn them over faster than Schwartz's.

Decisions, decisions. While Diamond pondered, Silva pulled out a fax from the organizers of the 2004 Capitale Européenne de la Culture conference in Lille, France. The French ministry of culture, no less, wanted Schwartz's to cater this prestigious event. Organizers wanted to fly in Silva and the smoked meat. Only one hitch. There was an embargo on Canadian beef in France, thanks to Mad Cow disease fears.

Silva next pulled out a story from a U.S. ski magazine. It was a feature on the Jay Peak resort in Vermont. But the writer counseled skiers to take a sick day in which to make the two-hour drive to Montreal for—what else?—Schwartz's smoked meat.

Owner Hy Diamond in his "office"—a table at the back.
"There is only one Carnegie Hall. There is only one Pavarotti.
And there is only one Schwartz's."

A family tradition. Manager Frank Silva's father worked at Schwartz's for twenty years, retiring in 1991. Frank started in 1982.

The big sign on the outside window of the deli reads Charcuterie Hebraïque de Montréal, but near and far, everyone knows it simply as Schwartz's. Only the eagle-eyed can scope a much smaller Schwartz sign over the door. No matter, the place is enshrined in local lore.

As Diamond and Silva continued to ponder, longtime customer Irwin Miller approached. "Hy, you're driving me crazy," Miller spewed. "I want to keep my father Joe in Florida for a few more weeks, but he wants to come home. He just can't spend another day away from Schwartz's."

Joe Miller was 88 and had been a regular at Schwartz's since it opened.

So what's the big fuss? It's all about the meat, Diamond has always said. He brought over a plate of medium old-fashioned and examined it. "Take a bite," he implored. "No, not with mustard or bread," he admonished.

"Smoked meat is not unlike a fine wine," he rhapsodized. "All you need is the meat. Every brisket is different, although they have all been smoked and marinated here for at least ten days before being served. Without chemicals, either. This is all natural. This is an art."

Diamond then concluded that a decision to open a second Schwartz's was of such magnitude had to be decided democratically. Or so he reasoned. He sought to have readers of the Montreal *Gazette* voice their opinions in a poll.

When the dust settled and the votes were tabulated, 68 percent of those who participated in the poll felt Schwartz's should franchise downtown and beyond—even as far as Hong Kong and Australia. Diamond was taken aback.

It became abundantly clear that Montrealers and ex-Montrealers take their smoked meat seriously. And there is little doubt Schwartz's is the real deli deal. However, Diamond was still conflicted. So displaying the wisdom of Solomon, Diamond decided to toss Montrealers a carrot—actually, a karnatzel—in terms of a compromise. He would expand Schwartz's catering services, which would mean a moveable deli feast could now be but a phone call away.

Diamond would dispatch entire smoked-meat briskets far and wide to those craving a Schwartz's original. The only catch is that Diamond would not let the meat go without one of his experienced cutters. So take note, those in deli-deprived Toronto and Vancouver, a similar arrangement could be made—with the cost of transport tacked on.

The decision not to expand was difficult. Diamond was tantalized with offers from potential downtown landlords, as well as those from around the country, willing to build him the deli of his dreams, down to a facsimile of the original Main smokehouse and grill and ceramic tiles. And one doesn't need a degree from the London School of Economics to realize Diamond could have become a very rich man had he agreed to franchise.

In the end, though, it came down to tradition. "When do you get the chance to become a part of Montreal history? Being on the Main has allowed us to serve both the city's east and west," said Diamond, chewing on a plate of smoked meat—no bread, no mustard—at his customary back table at Schwartz's. "I was simply overwhelmed by the response. But we're one of a kind and, to stay that way, the staff and I decided there could only be one location.

"Besides, how could we ever duplicate the aroma and the ambiance—such as it is—and the smokehouse? And the grill, which was bought second-hand seventy-six years ago. Sure, I was torn and tempted, but the feeling was, such a move could dilute the product. Worse, if customers didn't like the new location, it could kill us altogether."

Diamond then repeated his favourite mantra: "There is only one Carnegie Hall. There is only one Pavarotti. And there is only one Schwartz's."

Diamond and manager Silva are most unflinching on occasion, be it on franchising or taking liberties with the menu, which means woe to those who saunter into Schwartz's and have the temerity to ask for their smoked meat on white bread with mayo.

The massive response to the *Gazette* survey, both pro- and anti-expansion, also flew in the face of current health-food trends and diets. Even the brainiacs at Atkins who have deemed bacon better than some veggies would draw the line at a coronary-inducing, medium old-fashioned smoked-meat sandwich. Then again, lineups outside Schwartz's, even in the morning on the most bitterly cold winter day, would seem to suggest that Montrealers and tourists are willing to pay any dietary price for deli. And to read the praises from food-writers and celebs, you'd swear cholesterol was all some myth.

Hell, even those ever-health-conscious Rolling Stones— OK, perhaps not Keith Richards—insisted on Schwartz's smoked meat plus a cutter for their backstage nosh after their 2003 Bell Centre concert in Montreal. Doubtless, Mick Jagger and sidekick "Keef" could be among the many to applaud Diamond's decision that only one deli on the planet will ever bear the outdoor sign that reads "Charcuterie Hébraïque de Montréal"— even if no one has ever called it that.

Diamond was moved not just by the huge number of people who participated in the poll, but by their conviction. From faraway Chapel Hill, North Carolina, John Allore sounded off with a missive Diamond could relate to: "Don't mess with Schwartz's!!! You'll unravel the cosmic fabric of the universe!!!"

"Schwartz's is a landmark in Montreal. Leave well enough alone!" begged Richard Faucher of suburban Laval.

Then came the plaintive plea of an ex-Montrealer, identified only as Smoked Meat Nut, from Whitby, Ontario: "Never mind another location in Montreal. ... we need a Schwartz's in Toronto. Since moving from Montreal, I miss my smoked meat. Schwartz's would clean up here. Toronto has no idea what food is about. Even their so-called bagels here are nothing more than hardened plaster."

More reinforcement from Toronto came with this appeal from John Jepson: "TORONTO next. PLEASE! Half a million ex-Montrealers lined up at your door when you open. Give us a reason to live again!"

One Robbie Michaelson from restaurant-rich San Francisco made his pitch: "Schwartz's should open here, a city of great restaurants and lousy delis! People would line up from Fisherman's Wharf to Union Square for the true taste of smoked meat on rye!"

From Chicago, another ex-Montrealer, Gary Crawford, stated: "Yes! Schwartz's on Crescent is an excellent idea. However, the owners must—and this is a must—re-create the decor (or lack of same) of the one on the Main. None of this sleek, all in black, high-society Schwartz's. We—all Montrealers—won't bite. We just want Schwartz's II like the original. Then ... they can open up a third one down here on Chicago's Michigan Ave.!"

But from New York City, Tom had some chilling words: "Please, do not open another Schwartz's. What makes it special is its uniqueness. (As with) anything worth waiting for, real Montrealers don't mind standing outside in freezing midwinter weather to get a fix. Don't turn it into the another Starbucks, McDonald's, or, God forbid, Nickels."

And all the way from Iqaluit, Nunavut in the North came this memory from Kalman Strauss: "I can remember as a child, my grandfather would take my two brothers and me to Schwartz's almost every Sunday evening for a steak or smoked meat. There can only ever be one Schwartz's! But if I could choose a second location for Schwartz's, it would have to be in Iqaluit."

But perhaps Winnipeg resident and deli fan Shael Glesby had summed it up the best: "May the Schwartz be with you!"

João Gonçalves has been cutting smoked meat
for over thirty years.

[Three]

Montreal's Melting Pot

To UNDERSTAND SCHWARTZ'S place in the cosmos, one must understand the Main, its home since the dawn of this deli. The Main is the accepted moniker for St. Laurent Boulevard (once called St. Lawrence Boulevard) which is considered the geographical epicentre of Montreal. Actually, it's more a cultural than geographical epicentre. It is the boulevard that has stood as Montreal's own Mason-Dixon Line, the dividing point between anglophones to the west, francophones to the east and immigrant allophones smack in the middle of the Main. Though these geographical axioms no longer apply in modern-day Montreal, they did up until the middle of the last century. But the Main then served, as it still does today, as Montreal's melting pot, where anglos, francos and allos all converge.

While St. Laurent Boulevard just about stretches from one end of the city to the other, the Main generally refers to the area bounded by Sherbrooke Street to the south and Mount Royal Avenue to the north. But to purists, the true centre of the Main is the slice of St. Laurent Boulevard between Pine Avenue and Napoleon. And this is the area that's home to Schwartz's.

The Main has undergone a spectacular transformation over the last 30 years. Gone are the big garment factories and most of the mom-and-pop shops and the butchers, bakers and candlestick makers. In their place are trendy boutiques and edgy bars, high-end restos and high-tech software creators, and high-ceilinged lofts for well-heeled artistes. What was once Old World simple has become Old World chic. The charm is still there, but the accent is more on funky mishmash than plebian mishmash. In lieu of urbanite revolutionaries singing the praises of Marx, there are urbanite hipsters singing the praises of *The Matrix*.

About all that hasn't changed over the decades is Schwartz's, as well as its neighbours Moishe's Steak House (née Moishe's Romanian Paradise) and L. Berson and Son, the monument makers. Time has stood still at Schwartz's. And that time could still pass as the 1930s or '40s. And young and old, cool and square, anglo, franco and allo customers can all at least agree that Schwartz's should stay true to its cluttered roots.

Curiously, though, the Main, so synonymous with Montreal's rich multicultural history, was in the 1860s and '70s the primarily francophone community of St. Jean Baptiste. But toward the end of the century, Jewish, Portuguese, Greek, Italian and Eastern European immigrants flocked to the district, forever changing its makeup. The immigrants came to work the clothing factories and, to accommodate their needs, others set up small grocery stores, clothing shops, restaurants and social clubs.

Flash-forward to the twenty-first century. The Main offici-ally celebrated its 100th birthday in 2005. To commemorate the occasion and honour the immigrants who set up shop here, Montreal Mayor Gérald Tremblay found a little over $11 million in the municipal budget to beautify the Main with flowers and trees, wider sidewalks and better street lighting.

As it is, the Main, on some levels, bears little resemblance to the boulevard it once was. It has now morphed into a cultural spectacle that has something for everyone. For two weekends every summer, the Main is transformed into the city's most popular pedestrian boulevard, where autos are verboten. These days are aptly called Main Madness—Frénesie de la "Main." A carnival spirit prevails. Rollerbladers roll amok, flipping head over heels, occasionally butting heads with one another. Tam-tam troupes bang merrily. A makeshift sandy beach rises out of the asphalt to allow nubile professional men and women volley-ball players in the most revealing Spandex attire to bang away at their favourite sport. And families lounge in comfy sofas to catch Andy Warhol movies on a giant outdoor screen.

It's a special kind of madness happening. It's not just the everyday collision of ethnic cultures in the city's famed melting pot. It's an all-encompassing festival, where citizens forget about matters political and financial and soak the party spirit so contagious in Montreal in the summer.

The Main is, and has been, the perfect backdrop for a plethora of parties: the International Fringe Festival, the rival Infringement Festival, myriad movie festivals as well as the St. Laurent Boulevard Merchants Festival's Main Madness. Oh, and let's not forget what some cynics—guilty as charged—have labeled the Euro-trash Festival, wherein visitors from abroad with deep pockets descend upon the city in early June to partake in the F-1 mayhem that is the Canadian Grand Prix. While the driving boys in their fast toys spin around a racetrack in the southern regions of the city by day, they and their fans soak up the ambiance on the Main by night.

The cumulative result of all these meshings of humanity brings new meaning to circus—particularly in the town that gave rise to the world-renowned Cirque du Soleil. On any corner, you can catch thespians performing guerrilla theatre, or cinephiles discoursing on the merits of Louis Malle, or Frank Vitale's *Montreal Main*, that gritty 1974 movie ode to the boulevard. And, of course, merchants moving everything from sandals to sausages, tacky towels to exotic teas.

It's a scene—even in a city accustomed to outrageous costume dramas. These are field days for people-watchers. Fellini—who was second to none in casting unforgettable faces and figures—would have marvelled at the selection of street people.

Shirley Stewart is typical of the many Montrealers who've come to embrace this carnival on the Main. The feisty senior has volunteered for duty at the Fringe festival beer tent, where her clientele comes in a variety of ages, backgrounds and hair colours. "It's magical," she says. "People just come together so peacefully."

Diana Dent and Deb Pickman, two actors from England, are equally ebullient. They're impressed with the city's tolerance level. Both star in the Fringe fest satire *The Happy Cunt*, a rollicking feminist romp whose posters they've been allowed to hang. "This is a very hip town," says Dent. "Our play is raunchy and radically wicked, but it's done with humor, and audiences understand that."

Michael Rayner and Moira Quick, the Orlando, Florida-based stars of *Where are the Hands*, are also trying to ward off dehydration in the Fringe beer tent. They describe their show as a pseudo-drama about detachable runaway hands and kitchen utensils. "This street is just so unbelievable. It's long. It's linear. And people sell stuff on it," Quick deadpans.

"And the Portuguese custard tarts are unlike any I've ever had," interjects Pickman. "And the men and women are as captivating and exotic as I've ever seen," offers Dent.

Even for Montrealer Michael Wener, director of the sci-fi caper *The Scions of Hydra* at the Fringe fest, the atmosphere on the Main is something of a revelation. "It's a timeless scene. It's the bazaar and the bizarre. It's people hawking stuff and gawking at each other. It's great!"

"It's sublime," Pickman says. "It's like being on a pirate ship."

[Top] Manager Frank Silva and members of the B.C. Lions football team.[Bottom] If the walls could speak!

Non-performing visitors are also lapping up all the fun. San Franciscans Tammy Karpenko and her mother, Norma, believe they've hit the tourist mother lode on the Main.

A few blocks away at another pit stop for suds, noted Montreal movie director Léa Pool is waxing poetic. "This is magnificent. We always say that cinema is life and life is cinema, and here we have living proof on this street."

Meanwhile, John Ghrayeb, who is selling textiles at an outdoor stall, doesn't know what to make of the scene. "People are buying more, but I keep thinking that I'm part of some giant circus."

And at Schwartz's, smoked-meat cutter Costas Leventis reports business has been just decent. "Sure, it would be better if our regulars could park their cars close by, but we can afford to suffer a little to let people enjoy this weather."

"The problem is that it's too hot and we don't sell beer," says Schwartz's ever-philosophic manager Frank Silva. "But I really believe that smoked meat and theatre make for a beautiful marriage."

Tam-tam drummer Ahmadou Fadilou Ngom confirms Silva's assertion. The Senegalese musician and his entourage have begun to play next to the outdoor tables set up in front of Schwartz's for the occasion.

"I think it's a smart move, because even if you're from Senegal you quickly learn that in Montreal everyone likes to come to Schwartz's," suggests Ngom. "I must confess that I eat there all the time myself, too. The secret is that drummers need lots of meat—the spicier the better—to perform well."

Silva smiles, then chimes: "I truly believe that many of the problems of the world could be resolved over a smoked-meat sandwich."

He just may be right. Folks would be too full to fight.

Four

They Fought the Law, and the Law Won

THROUGH THE FIRST FIFTY YEARS of its existence, Schwartz's had little trouble with the law. Indeed, the law—that is, lawyers, prosecutors, judges, cops and even politicos who create laws— have always been among Schwartz's most regular patrons, which couldn't have hurt. Even the calorie and cholesterol police cut the deli a break.

But in 1976, Schwartz's, and every other deli and steakhouse in the province of Quebec, had to comply with an ordinance from the food police. They all had to cease and desist from serving their steaks on wooden platters. Platters which seemed to enhance the sizzle of the steaks—the red juices of the meat streaming along the platter and finding temporary shelter in the wooden crevices—served almost as works of art, the ultimate homage. Yet overly finicky or not, our food police opted for caution, pointing out that bacteria from the steaks could also find temporary shelter on the wooden platters and that the bacteria was so ingrained that no amount of washing and scrubbing could extricate it. And this was before the days of Mad Cow disease. In retrospect, a prudent decision from the food inspectors—even if nothing beats carving a rib on a wooden platter.

Still, this episode positively pales when compared to Schwartz's skirmishes with the province's language police. (Yup, Quebec must have more cops per capita than any fiefdom on the planet.) A little history is in order here. The Government of

Quebec had passed a law called Bill 101 to ensure that the French language would survive on this continent. Well and good. Sacrifices had to be made. Schwartz's, like Eaton's and Steinberg's, would have to lose their apostrophes in the new scheme of things. Initially, Schwartz's kept its apostrophe "s," but added "Charcuterie Hébraïque de Montréal" to its outdoor sign. Eventually, though, deli management thought it best not to disrupt the peace and upset any patrons, and lost the apostrophe "s" on its smaller outside sign over the door. No matter, because Schwartz's, like Kleenex and Kodak, was so ingrained in the consciousness of locals and tourists, anglos, francos and allos alike that it has always been referred to by the last name of its founder, apostrophe included. Current owner Hy Diamond can't recall anyone ever asking him directions to Charcuterie Hébraïque de Montréal.

Similarly, neither Diamond, nor any of Schwartz's managers, past or present, can ever recall anyone sauntering into the deli and demanding *boeuf mariné*. This is where the language laws start getting a tad arcane and inane. With the creation of Bill 101 came the Office de la langue française (OLF) and its cadre of language marshalls to uphold the law. Commonly referred to as the Tongue Troopers in certain cynical quarters in the province, these language cops were hellbent to enforce one of the offshoots of the law. Specifically, the one that dared to translate smoked meat into *viande fumée*. Under the French menu aspect of the law, it was deemed that smoked meat wasn't really smoked, or *fumée*, largely because it was marinated in spices before spending a brief time in a smokehouse. Furthermore, the law declared that smoked meat wasn't really meat, or *viande*. Rather, it was beef—or *boeuf*. Hence, *boeuf mariné*.

Problem is that no one—franco, anglo or allo—could come to grips with the French term. Of the millions of sandwiches sold at Schwartz's, no one working there can recall anyone asking for a medium-fat *boeuf mariné* with double mustard.

Realizing that the masses wouldn't cotton to the expression, the Office de la langue française has since decided that *viande fumée* will suffice and is no longer verboten. And what was to prove even more galling to the Office was the declaration by the *Dictionnaire Robert*, the ultimate authority on the French language in Paris, that "un smoked meat" qualified as a bona fide French Canadian dish. So it is written in *Le Robert Québécois*, their dictionary dedicated to North American French. That really must bite when one is proven to be more Catholic than the Pope.

For his part, Diamond breathes a sigh of relief that no one has ever undertaken to translate that mass of artery-clogging fat, trimmed from the brisket, called spek, a word for which none of the official language groups wish to take any credit.

This wasn't the last of Schwartz's brushes with the Tongue Troopers. In April 1996, then-Quebec Premier Lucien Bouchard, another regular Schwartz's nosher and smoked-meat aficionado, stopped by for lunch. Not far away from him was a photographer for the Montreal daily *Le Devoir*. He not only caught Bouchard in the process of scarfing down a smoked-meat sandwich, but also directly in front of a sign that was in flagrant violation of Bill 86. According to this law, signage, inside and outside commercial establishments in the province, had to display the French words at least twice the size of the English. And there was our Premier Bouchard, happily tucking into a smoked-meat sandwich completely oblivious to the illegal signage behind him: Extra Charge Per Shared Meal. Both French and English were the same size.

Quel horreur!! Well, it didn't take long for an alert and anonymous reader of *Le Devoir*—and not Bouchard—to file a

Grill man and cutter Jason LeBrun.

Waiter Pablo Quintero with an order of fries—some of the best in town.
But don't expect them to come with mayo.

complaint with the Office de la langue française. A language cop was dispatched to the deli and notified management that it would have to change about twenty of its indoor signs in order that French be double the size of the English writing on them. Rather than risk the wrath of the Office and engage in an endless and futile battle, Schwartz's management complied and spent about a thousand dollars to change the offending signs.

Diamond agrees that rocking the language boat would have been pointless. "All the same, it is ironic that one of the few places in the city which bridges east and west, English and French, should get caught up in this kind of situation," he says. "No matter what kind of language battles were being fought around us, there has always been harmony here. The only thing customers ever complain about is waiting for tables—but they do that equally in both languages."

Those were interesting days in Quebec, particularly for those who relished the prospect of life imitating the art of Eugene Ionesco.

There was another flap that made Montreal front-page news around the planet. The good folks from the Office de la langue française donned their plus-fours, er, *plus-quatres,* and issued a twenty-seven-page edict on what constitutes proper French on the golf course. They fretted that golf was becoming too English and, therefore, the proper terminology for a birdie in Quebec would be a *oiselet* and that a driver would be a *bois numero un.* Failure to comply could lead to the guillotine in the *fosse d'herbe*—grass bunker, silly.

This is not to suggest that some of us don't appreciate the efforts of the OLF to inject a little levity into our otherwise humdrum lives. After all, better to make the news for infractions relating to fracturing the French language than for armed insurrection.

Diamond, the ever glass-half-full guy, says these sort of squabbles are a small price to pay for living in the most laid-back metropolis on the planet. "The reality is that government bureaucrats don't have much impact on the lives of most Montrealers. I can't ever recall a dust-up at Schwartz's relating to the language of the signs or service. The fact is we can serve customers in a dozen different languages, if need be—including French and English."

Indeed, Diamond is so hell-bent on ensuring that Schwartz's retains its place as bridge between cultures that he organized what is believed to be a first on the fundraising front in Montreal. Diamond reached out to the English and French communities in the city to join forces on the battle to beat ovarian cancer. "People always seem to focus on the negative or petty in this city, but not enough is made of the camaraderie that binds us all."

[Five]

A Laughing Matter

MAYBE IT HAS SOMETHING to do with the gas they both induce. But deli and comedy have gone hand-in-hand since Laurel and Hardy started slapping each other silly at the turn of the century. In comedy central, New York City, the big players—the agents and producers—knock back pastrami sandwiches at the Stage or Second Avenue delis, while getting the goods on up-and-comers and trading dirt on has-beens. The scene was immortalized in Woody Allen's comedy *Broadway Danny Rose*. Well, Montreal plays its own version of *Broadway Danny Rose* every summer at the Just for Laughs festival.

For more years than they can remember, Rick, Lou, Chuck, Danny, Howard and other heavyweights from the humour field have taken time out from the comedy festival and have been meeting at Schwartz's to gobble some smoked meat—the far superior Montreal equivalent to pastrami—and to gossip. Especially to gossip. They're at the comedy festival on the look-out for raw meat—talent—to represent, to book onto the Letterman and Leno late-night shows, and to sign for movie deals. Talent that might make them rich, or merely give them more heartburn.

These New Yorkers are a spirited lot. Often they're funnier than the comics they represent. "Have I found anything yet at the festival?" asks the slick Rick Newman, founder of the Catch a Rising Star comedy-club emporium in the U.S., and agent of the abrasive Allan Havey. "Yeah, I found a twenty-dollar bill in my hotel room. But it was Canadian. What's that worth?"

"Sure, ya find things here," counters Lou Viola, an agent for Agency of Performing Arts (APA), which has represented everyone from Michael (Kramer) Richards to Steven Wright. "We already know about 90 percent of the American talent, but we find Australians, Brits and Canadians.

"I found one of those Australians in my hotel the other night, and told him to get the hell out!" Viola adds between mouthfuls of smoked meat. "In the past, we've been able to introduce the British comedy community to America."

But there's a price to pay. "You have to hang out in the bars till three in the morning with those guys, and get as drunk as they do."

Drinking always brings out the best dirt, even better than smoked meat. "The only people who drink more than the Brit comics and the members of the press are the Brit musicians," claims APA agent Danny Robinson, who discovered Canadian comic Mike MacDonald at the comedy festival years ago.

"Most of the good acts are already represented when they come here, but the Montreal festival is the place you go to see who's going to break out," Robinson says.

"And then there's the people we forever ostracize after seeing them here," says Howard Lapides, Mike MacDonald's manager.

Though their native New York City might seem a more logical setting for a comedy festival-cum-shmoozathon, the guys say it hasn't worked there.

"They once tried a comedy festival in New York and it was monumentally unnoticed," Viola says. "This is a town that just seems to lend itself to festivals. Hell, if tidal waves, earthquakes and volcanos don't get the attention of New Yorkers, what chance did their comedy festival have?"

The consensus here is the comedy biz is in trouble. "The comedy clubs are closing or are on the verge of closing in New York," Newman says.

"It's way too much comedy on TV. That's the problem," Lapides says.

"Yeah, there's just an over-abundance of standups on the tube," shrugs Viola.

Though they've all handled stars who soar, none know what the magic ingredient is that goes into the making of one.

"Would we be sitting here if we knew?" Newman says. "It's the X factor."

"It's not us who decide," explains Robinson. "It's the public. Look, there's comedians like Gilbert Gottfried or Dana Gould whom we love, but they're just too hip for the room."

And then there's the amazing success story of Michael Richards, who rose to stardom as the wacked-out neighbor on the Seinfeld TV series and who has also hosted a Just for Laughs gala.

"Kramer is a confluence of the right script, the right role and the right actor at the right time," says Viola. "What agents do with talent is a lot like making sausages; you don't want to see it until it's ready."

Time out for a little snack. Plates of steaming smoked meat, rye bread, fries, coleslaw, pickles and peppers are unceremoniously plopped on the table. "This is the time we complain there's way too much smoked meat on the table—but in the end it will all be gone," Lapides predicts. "It always is."

Between mouthfuls, it's now time to dredge up dirt from festivals past: "Remember that ring-tosser who came on after the Bubble Boy and Mike MacDonald years ago? He's now flipping burgers in L.A.," Viola says. "Remember the guy with the dog act who shoved his finger..."

"This is the time we stop eating," blurts a disgusted-looking Lapides. "I'm gonna be sick."

Charles Joffe appears in Schwartz's doorway and makes his way through the throngs. Joffe is the dean of all agents and scouts. He manages Woody Allen, and he has represented Robin Williams, Billy Crystal and David Letterman. When Joffe talks, the others stop eating. Now that's respect.

Joffe declares that festival performers David Cross and Lea DeLaria—the first openly lesbian comedian—are destined to "break."

"Montreal is the best comedy showcase anywhere," Joffe says. "It's the one event the American comedy industry most looks forward to. And it has among the best talent, and audiences, I've ever seen."

And much of that talent these Americans have caught comes from Canada. "I don't think Canadians realize their comedians are the funniest in the world," Lapides says.

"Canadians have a complex. Until a Canadian act breaks out in the U.S., they won't be accepted at home."

They toss back names: Mike MacDonald, Mike Myers, Martin Short, Catherine O'Hara.

"Australians, on the other hand, aren't funny. That goes without saying," Lapides adds.

But these guys aren't North American chauvinists. They respect comedians from around the world.

"Language and country aren't important," suggests Joffe. "Jacques Tati and Marcel Marceau are two of the funniest performers ever—and they never said a word."

"Mind you, there aren't many funny comedians from Bermuda," Robinson says. "And the Jamaicans have the good sense to stick to music."

"There aren't too many funny Germans out there, because

we don't let them in," Newman quips.

Despite the fact they can sling one-liners with the best of them—around this Formica table, anyway—nobody here desires to change careers.

"Wanna know how long a minute is?" Viola asks. "Get up on stage."

OK, enough about comedy. What about our smoked meat?

"I like it," Lapides says. "But fact is Montreal smoked meat hasn't broken. We've had bad comedians from here break out faster than Montreal smoked meat in the States. Still, Schwartz's is the gotta-come-to spot in town."

"They named a sandwich after us at a New York deli," Joffe says in reference to *Broadway Danny Rose*, which he produced.

"I don't want to hurt feelings here," Lapides adds, "but this still can't compare to Second Avenue Deli pastrami. This is overblown corned beef. Maybe if they learned to cut it properly."

Fighting words. A waiter overhears the shot. He is incensed. He seems ready to toss down the gauntlet—or perhaps a karnatzel. But he is quickly restrained by another waiter.

Oblivious to the backstage drama, the managers and agents continue chomping. Conversation switches from smoked meat to Joffe's prized client Allen.

"Woody's not here because Soon-Yi isn't into smoked meat," Newman cracks, in reference to Allen's significant other.

"Ya know," Joffe bellows, "not one Canadian has been so impolite as to say something nasty about Woody. Just this American schmuck!"

"Hey, it's a comedy festival," Newman counters.

"It would be great to see Woody back with Keaton in an old-fashioned comedy," Joffe continues.

"That's right, Buster Keaton hasn't worked in years, but when Woody calls ..." Lapides cracks.

"Wanna know what comedy is? Tragedy plus timing," says Joffe.

Perhaps. But ya wanna know what else comedy is? Watching the agents and scouts scramble out of Schwartz's and leave the last guy sitting—festival boss Andy Nulman—to pick up the bill.

"Hey, that's what show biz is all about," Robinson beams.

Comic Jackie Mason with owner Hy Diamond.

Six

Unofficial Doorman

It's teeming outside. But this doesn't prevent Ryan Larkin from assuming his regular daytime post by Schwartz's entrance. "Rain or shine, hot or cold, I have a mission to be here," says Larkin, sixty-one going on twenty-one. "People depend on me, damn it." (Larkin had been Schwartz's official unofficial doorman for over a decade before he passed away in 2007.)

Larkin is as synonymous with the Main as Schwartz's. And their's is a marriage more bizarre than anything any fiction writer could have ever concocted.

Larkin just may be the world's only Oscar-nominated "doorman." In the late 1960s and early '70s, Larkin was considered one of the world's most innovative animators and was up for an Academy Award in 1969 for his short *Walking*. But life eventually got in the way. Larkin battled the bottle, drugs and personal demons. He lost most everything, including his job at the National Film Board of Canada (NFB), and ended up panhandling on the Main by day and sleeping in the nearby Old Brewery Mission by night. He now follows a regular daily routine. After opening doors at Schwartz's for spare change and all the fries from within he can eat, he moves across the street in the afternoon to the Copacabana bar to trade his cash for brew, 'cuz, like Mr. Bojangles, he still drinks a bit. But he hasn't abandoned his artistic muse. He created the logo, a cartoon character called Bango, for the Main's 100th anniversary poster.

Larkin has been in a particularly buoyant mood of late. A

couple of months back, an animated offering about his life, appropriately called *Ryan*, took home the Oscar for its maker Chris Landreth. Larkin was, natch, nursing brews over at the Copacabana when the Academy Award was announced that cold February night. Director Landreth brought the house down at the Copa when he received the Oscar and offered this explanation for his award on the podium in Hollywood: "The grace and humility of one guy watching in Montreal. Ryan Larkin, I dedicate this award to you."

Larkin, rarely at a loss for words, was speechless. His cronies and former NFB cohorts, sitting next to him, were nearly reduced to tears. Many victory shots were consumed. The 14-minute *Ryan* is not only the story of Larkin's rise and fall presented in 3-D computer animation, but is also a plea on behalf of director Landreth for Ryan to abandon the bottle and get back to work.

Larkin pledges to do one out of two. He announces that he is working on a new film, *Spare Change*, which will offer another take on his existence. He also announces to one and all that he spent the hours leading up to the Oscar gala opening doors in front of Schwartz's. "Oscars or not, I can't forego my regular work," he says. "So many lives will be thrown out of whack if I don't open doors at Schwartz's. These are my children. I can't disappoint them, can I?"

Inside Schwartz's this day, life is almost as chaotic as it is outside with the rain-drenched Larkin spouting philosophy to the equally rain-drenched in line. The waiters joke among themselves that it's perhaps time to contemplate the construction of an ark. The waiters are also shvitzing something fierce. An electrical problem in the kitchen has cut off some power. As a consequence, on a day when the temperature is somewhere north of 30 degrees Celsius—and north of 40, when

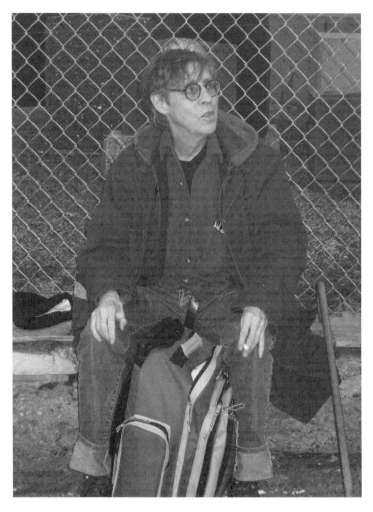

Ryan Larkin sitting in front of L. Berson Monuments.

the humidity is factored in—there is no air conditioning at Schwartz's. And owing to the fact that power has disrupted the dishwasher, there is no silverware, plates or glasses available to customers. Instead, there are plastic dishes and cutlery and styrofoam cups. To further add insult, there are no fries today. Owner Hy Diamond's simple "oy" says it all.

And yet, come noon, the faithful have lined up outside in the heat and the humidity and the pouring rain. And no one complains when told there won't be fries today. On the other hand, when Morris the repairman surfaces, people point fingers and ask if there might be air conditioning before the onset of winter. Morris wisely walks on.

Montreal film-maker Kevin Tierney insists he's Irish, but a bar mitzvah is all that separates him from the Jewish clientele at his table. "I come for a little meat and a little vegetable," he kibitzes, after taking his seat. The meat would be smoked, and the vegetable would be a half-sour pickle. Details.

"I need my salt and my salt," he adds, wiping sweat from his brow. "It keeps me pumped, and the makers of Lipitor happy. Hello! Could it get any hotter in here? Now this is what you call customer loyalty. I get soaked trying to make it into the place. And I get more soaked just sitting here."

Stanley Lewis, the acclaimed sculptor, drops in from his atelier across the street which he rents from L. Berson & Son Cemetery Monuments. (Lewis had been a Schwartz's regular for more than sixty years until he passed away at seventy-six in 2006.)

He visits daily for a little shmooze and a plateful of fries. No fries today, Lewis is told. He remains stoical. "You have to accept the good with the bad in life," says the sculptor, before going on to discourse about Michelangelo.

Lewis is, frankly, uncertain whether Michelangelo would

Sculptor Stanley Lewis, a Schwartz's regular for almost sixty years, rents his studio from monument maker L. Berson & Son, across the street from Schwartz's.

have been a smoked-meat devotee. But he's certain Michelangelo had never shown one of his pieces at a deli. Lewis will. One of his pieces will soon be on display at this deli. This tickles Lewis no end.

"It's only fitting," he elaborates. "I remember coming here as a kid, when two sandwiches cost a quarter. The place had these barrels of pickles and herring. They say if you want to understand an art form, you have to go where it was created."

Apparently, an analogy between art and smoked meat is being drawn.

"But this is also a place full of mystery," Lewis adds. "Few people have ever been upstairs to see the smokehouse. Many have tried."

Lewis allows that the upstairs is almost as big a mystery as founder Reuben Schwartz. But no time for deep philosophy now. Lewis spots "Marky" Mark Saykaly entering the restaurant.

Some call "Marky" Mark Montreal's answer to Broadway Danny Rose, although he's more likely a mental dead ringer for Seinfeld's tightly wound George Costanza, or the man who inspired him, Larry David.

"Marky" Mark has been coming to Schwartz's for 50 years. Like me, he was turned on to the place as a five-year-old by his dad. He, too, would come prior to taking in an Alouettes game at Molson Stadium.

"My first memory was a little painful," he recalls. "I couldn't finish my smoked-meat sandwich. I felt I had failed."

His second memory was that he and his dad were sharing their table with strangers. Though not exactly a world-travelled gastronome at five, he had never been to a restaurant before where sharing a table with strangers was de rigueur. Oddly enough, years later, as a hormone-addled teen, "Marky" Mark would encourage the waiters to seat attractive young women strangers at his table. But that turns out to have triggered some major angst for Marky Mark.

"Here I am a good Lebanese boy doing my bit for world peace by eating karnatzels at Schwartz's," he says. "But, honestly, I was having trouble getting dates as a teen. Then it hit me: I should have been going to Schwartz's after trying to meet women, not before. My karnatzel-induced garlic breath was scaring all the girls away. No wonder I could never get a date. It was horrible, I tell you."

"Marky" Mark seems to have overcome this obstacle. Though a garmentologist by trade—specifically, lady's lingerie—he is quite the ham. He wanders into Schwartz's with a briefcase filled with jokes. Today's topic: perks of being over fifty.

"You have to look on the bright side here," "Marky" Mark opines. "For example, in a hostage situation, you are probably the first to be released."

Nice. "OK," he shoots back. "No one expects you to run ... anywhere. And how about this? There is nothing left to learn the hard way. Wait, there's more. You can live without sex, but not your glasses. And you enjoy hearing about other people's operations. Your supply of brain cells is finally down to a manageable size ..."

Stop, you're killing me.

"One more," he pleads. "The best perk of being over 50 is that you can't even remember who sent you this list in the first place."

"Marky" Mark likes the last one. But he stops giggling for a moment to delve into deli philosophy. He admits the allure of Schwartz's may be more the characters than the grub. He, too, is from and has worked in this 'hood all his life. "It's amazing who shows up here. Artists, punks, tourists, sinners, saints, actors. Really, though, it's more interesting at night. Then the real characters come. I met this sweet old Jewish lady one night. 'Such a nice boy,' she kept telling me. 'Are you sure you're not Jewish?' Sometimes I wonder."

This reminds "Marky" Mark of another joke he must share with the table. "Listen up. I'm a Leb, but I can relate to this one. A young Jewish man is overjoyed. He tells his mother he's fallen in love and that he's going to get married. He then asks his mother: 'Just for fun, Ma, I'm going to bring over three women and you try to guess which one I'm going to marry.' The mother goes along.

"The next day, the son brings over three gorgeous women and sits them down on the couch. The women start chatting with one another. Then the son says: 'OK, Ma, guess which one I'm going to marry?' The mother quickly replies: 'The one on the right.' The son says: 'That's amazing, Ma. How did you ever figure that out?' To which the Jewish mother replies: 'Simple, I don't like her.'"

"Marky" Mark is about to split a gut. "Come on, that was good, right?"

But as is his wont, "Marky" Mark is able to segue into a subject that has no bearing on what he was just talking about. He now recalls the days when the Main wasn't a one-way street. "Ah, such wonderful havoc when it was two-way," he recalls. "Cars were double-parked on both sides of the street as drivers would run in to pick up smoked meat. People would be stopped for so long that the hookers actually had time to solicit customers." And do... gosh knows what.

"Marky" Mark is a worrier. He worries that some may be turned off Schwartz's because it doesn't have desserts. And he worries that if Schwartz's did have desserts it would trigger other problems. "It's a real dilemma," he says, shaking his head. "It would be nice, but it would hurt the turnover factor. I stay up nights worrying about such things. Surprising?"

Not really. He says he's less a comedian than a would-be comedy writer. He figures he could have penned some dynamite Seinfeld scripts just hanging around Schwartz's. "Look at that gum machine next to the cash," he says. "Is it half-full? Or half-empty? Or has no one bought any gum balls in the last 50 years?"

This leads "Marky" Mark to a diatribe on the complexities of the English language that appear to baffle mostly him. "It's crazy when you think about it. Really, there is no egg in eggplant nor ham in hamburger. There is neither apple nor pine in pineapple. And English muffins weren't invented in England or French fries in France." The man is like a logic machine. He barely has time to come up for air, before adding: "Sweetmeats are candies while sweetbreads, which aren't sweet, are meat. Boxing rings are square and a guinea pig is neither from Guinea nor is it a pig. If the plural of goose is geese, why isn't more than one moose, meese? Or one index, two indices? How can a slim chance and a fat chance be the same, while a wise man and a wise guy are opposites? And if teachers taught, why didn't preachers praught? And if a vegetarian eats vegetables, what does a humanitarian eat?"

Somehow we all know that there would be some sort of method to "Marky" Mark's madness, that we would get back, in most circuitous fashion, to the raison d'être to this conversation. Here it is: "And how about this? We're eating smoked meat in the non-smoking section. Strange or what?"

A Schwartz's classic. A medium-fat sandwich, fries, coleslaw and red pepper, a half-sour pickle and the requisite black cherry soda.

[Seven]

The Shmutz Factor

THE SUN HAS SET. The night shift is on the job. And more deli debates ensue. Sheldon Chad, the writer of the vintage CBC-TV gumshoe series *Seeing Things*, is doing a little investigating himself. The smoked-meat maker Coorsh, he insists, started out as kosher—and hence the name. But the buzz is that it cost Coorsh too much to stay kosher, so it, too, went to the deli darkside. Then the company started to mass-produce the individual-sized, frozen smoked-meat packages.

So? "It's an integral part of Montreal smoked-meat history," Chad states.

Yeah, but the stuff tasted like putty with spice. "But it's all part of smoked-meat's evolution," Chad says.

Next it's on to a comparative analysis of Montreal delis. Chad rates Snowdon Deli high, mostly because of the fries. "Schwartz's has always had the shlep and the rep," he explains. "It's a killer combo."

Before bolting, Chad pledges to press his theory about an analogy between Schwartz's and Monty Python.

And speaking of Monty Python, I expect a farce to break out at any moment. A trio of Swiss folk have descended upon our table. One speaks French. One speaks English. One speaks German. The French speaker, Stéphane Wolf, is a computer-systems wonk and professor at the Univérsité de Montréal. He has become a Schwartz's habitué since moving here a few years ago. His two friends, Patrick and Eliza Meilleur, are first-time visitors to Montreal and Schwartz's. David Chalk, a Montreal barrister at our table, explains to the Meilleurs that smoked meat tastes something like their "Alsatian pickle-fleisch." They look at Chalk like he's just been plopped down on Earth from Planet Alsatian Pickle-Fleisch. They have no idea what he's talking about—in any language.

Eliza is a concert pianist. Patrick is a mathematician. They seem to get along well in spite of their respective vocations.

Also at the table is Chalk's partner in law, Ed Blanshay. He figures he's been coming to Schwartz's regularly for more years than he cares to remember, since leaving McGill law school. It wasn't easy at first. A friend had urged him to eat at Schwartz's. He told Blanshay it was on the Main near Moishe's. So Blanshay spent a considerable amount of time going up and down the Main in search of Schwartz's—but to no avail.

Several years later, his buddy told Blanshay he would take him to Schwartz's that night for dinner. Blanshay figured his friend was trying to put him on. Give it up, Blanshay said. "There is no Schwartz's. I spent hours looking for it a few years ago and I couldn't find it."

It was only after his friend personally escorted him there that night when Blanshay figured out why he could never find it. "The sign said Montreal Hebrew Delicatessen. I'm sure there was no mention of Schwartz's anywhere on the place."

Since that fateful night, it's been difficult to wrest Blanshay away from the deli.

But now a word from our Swiss tourists. The pianist loves it. The math dude simply says it's good. The computer wonk says friends either love it or hate it. But we all acknowledge the math dude would have been far more euphoric if he had not ordered his sandwich lean.

"That's a rookie mistake," Blanshay says. "Besides, it's a big misconception that fatty smoked meat is bad for you."

Drum roll, please. Now it can be told. Blanshay will soon be the official Schwartz's—or Montreal Hebrew Delicatessen—poster boy. Blanshay, you see, subscribes to one of the stranger diets known to man. It's a modified Atkins/Schwartz's regimen.

And I kibitz you not, ladies and spek-lovers, Blanshay has lost—another drum roll, please—a whopping 90 pounds over the last four years pigging out on smoked meat—the fatter, the better. Having known him before, I can vouch for the weight loss. And, really, why would anyone make such an outrageous claim unless it were true?

And yet it all seems so wrong, so unsavoury, coming to a cholesterol factory to lose weight. Even the normally neutral Swiss are alarmed. Stéphane, the computer whiz and prof, points out that Dr. Atkins is dead and was apparently obese at the time of his demise.

Chalk the barrister pipes in: "Ed lives!"

As for Blanshay, he merely says that Atkins's death was the result of a fall. In fairness, Blanshay may feast on the fatty smoked meat, but he manages to avoid the rye bread and the fries —no small task, either—and drinks only Diet Coke. He also stays away from pasta and desserts and excessive booze.

When he was a smoked-meat novice, he used to hang at a downtown deli. Then the deli moved and Blanshay says its smoked meat never recovered. After Schwartz's, Blanshay favours Abie's in the West Island 'burbs, then Lester's, a few minutes away from Schwartz's.

Chalk has been coming around to Schwartz's for the last thirty-two years. Not only does he swear by Blanshay's stunning weight loss, but he, too, has started to adhere to Blanshays modified Atkins/Schwartz diet. He's lost more than 30 pounds recently, simply by chowing down on fatty smoked meat, pickles and coleslaw.

Elvis with Johnny Haim, October 31, 1994.

"No one loved fries and bread more than me, but into every life comes a little sacrifice," he says, while cheerfully stuffing his face with smoked meat.

So what of spek? Blanshay and Chalk don't indulge often, but insist it's not verboten in their plan.

"Look, my health has never been better," Blanshay insists. Knock on Arborite. "I ski. I golf. I bike. I'm a changed man. Sure, they say fat closes arteries. But the body needs fat to convert to sugar. We're born with fat pouches that need to be filled with fat, then converted to sugar."

I'm getting a little nauseous now. Stéphane the math-man, though, is intrigued with Blanshay's theory. "The charm of Schwartz's is not unlike that of a little restaurant in the Swiss Alps where we eat well and fast."

And evidently where the waiters can be just as brusque. "One of my friends was taking his time eating at Schwartz's one night," Stéphane recalls. "There was a big lineup outside to get in, so the waiter actually told him not to chew his food, but rather to swallow it, to make him finish faster."

For no apparent reason, Chalk announces: "It's all about the shmutz. That's what makes the difference between Schwartz's and the other delis."

Sorry, I didn't bring my decoder ring. I ask Chalk to elaborate.

"It's elementary," he says. "It's the shmutz, the build-up of fat and spices and god knows what, in the smokehouse here that makes the difference. Almost 80 years of shmutz will do the trick every time. It's the same principle as wine. It's those old casks that give the vintage Bordeaux wines their edge."

"Ah, shmutz," repeats the pianist Eliza, like she has just undergone one of life's great epiphanies.

"More to the point," Chalk continues, "it's the lack of shmutz that has killed Schwartz's competition. But that's really why Schwartz's could never franchise. The quality would never be the same in a new smokehouse ... "

Don't tell me, because of the shmutz.

"Right," says Chalk. "And that's precisely why American pastrami can never measure up to Schwartz's smoked meat: shmutz!"

Chalk is on a roll now. He would like Schwartz's owner Hy Diamond to do with Blanshay what Subway did with Jared, that odd fellow who claims he lost hundreds of pounds simply sucking back submarine sandwiches—with bread. "I can see it now," Chalk marvels. "No more, what would Jared do? No, the new mantra for our generation will be: "What would Ed do?"

Jerry Silverman, working the cash this evening, overhears

the conversation and can see the possibilities of a modified Atkins/Schwartz Blanshay diet. "The lineups will be around the city when people get wind of the diet," he says.

I'm thinking a lard Lourdes here. Silverman is thinking Schwartz's will need another couple of cashiers working to handle the throngs.

Silverman has been a cashier here the last twenty years. This is not his chosen vocation. Prior to entering the hallowed deli, Silverman was a radio disk jockey, doing the coveted morning shtick at CFMB in the city. OK, so CFMB is an ethnic radio station, and Silverman—he actually called himself Jay Silver back then—found himself sandwiched (no pun intended) between the Hindu Half-Hour and the heavy-metal strains of Vomit and the Zits.

"Stuff happens. Life changes," Silverman philosophizes. "Plus, I've met some of the biggest stars in show-biz at the cash." Céline Dion, a regular when in town, even addresses Silverman by name. Jackie Mason doesn't, but he's not complaining.

Silverman has also met a slew of Canadian prime ministers at his post: Pierre Trudeau, Jean Chrétien and, most recently, Paul Martin. "All decent fellows," Silverman observes.

But Silverman is invariably the bearer of bad news for some. It causes him some anguish to have to tell cash-strapped customers that Schwartz's doesn't accept credit cards. "At least, we now have a cash-dispensing machine next to the bathrooms," he says.

It also chagrins him to tell folks on the phone that Schwartz's doesn't take reservations. "That's my role," he says. "The waiters see all the happy people. But I have to deal with those in distress."

Definitely not in distress is customer Tommy Yee, paying his bill. Reared in the area, Yee has since moved to Toronto where he works for a branch of the United Nations. His first stop when he comes back for a visit is Schwartz's. "What's not to like here?" he asks, sounding more like my grandmother than the Dalai Lama. "In fact, I'm shlepping this take-out back to Toronto. There's nothing like this in Toronto. Oy, it's all about franchises there. Schwartz's is all about soul."

Sure enough, though, the next customer who comes to Silverman's cash pulls out a credit card to pay. "What?" the customer shoots back, looking like he's about to hurl the smoked meat sandwich he just ate. "I have no cash."

Silverman points him to the ATM in the back. "In the end, they all pay," he says. "And in the end, the place has never been robbed, either."

Silverman's most vivid memory on the job is not joyous. He had broken his leg one day and a former Schwartz's manager, a slave-driver, demanded that he come into work that night, or else. Silverman was in agony, but he showed up.

He can eat all the smoked meat he wants, but he doesn't anymore. His cholesterol went up as a consequence, so he keeps his distance from the meat.

Forget Céline Dion or Jackie Mason. Silverman is about to touch base with another show-biz icon. There is a huge commotion at the door. Cameras are clicking. Cell phones are popping out of pockets. Customers are craning their necks. It is the ageless Joan Rivers, fresh from a command performance at the Just for Laughs festival, making her debut at Schwartz's. She has been told that before hightailing it back to the Left Coast her mission to Montreal is not complete. She must chow down on Montreal smoked meat.

Rivers, fully prepared for her Schwartz's baptism, is holding court, surrounded by friends from the biz, a couple of media interlopers and Schwartz's boss Hy Diamond. Rivers regales all with hilarious tales relating to the storage of ashes of deceased

Joan Rivers with Hy Diamond.
"Fully prepared for her Schwartz's baptism."

Mike Nelli, one of the two night managers, was at the helm when former Prime Minister Paul Martin paid a surprise visit with his entourage.

loved ones, including dogs, taking up nearly all her cupboard space. Next she's waxing witty about her exploits on Celebrity Family Feud, wherein the Rivers clan battled the Wayne Newton brood. She also tries to show compassion to members of Overeaters Anonymous: "Who are they trying to kid? Anonymous? Their rallying cry is Save the Whales... for breakfast."

Since her husband passed away in 1987, Rivers has had few men in her life but she insists she's not complaining. Much. "There was one fellow I really wanted to keep around, but he died a couple of months ago and I figured he would have started to smell." Pause. "Besides, there wouldn't have been much conversation, either."

Customers and staff, caught in the middle, howl, taking in Rivers's impromptu shtick. Almost lost in the shuffle—and no doubt grateful for that—is ex-federal foreign affairs minister Maxime Bernier, knocking back a sandwich at the counter with an engaging female companion—not Julie Couillard, the woman with the uninvestigated past who created a furor after reporting that he had left secret government intelligence papers at her home. Bernier comes over to the Rivers table, between bites, to ask film producer Kevin Tierney if he'd be interested in making a movie, from, Bernier's, and not Couillard's, point of view. Bernier is then introduced to Rivers, who, no doubt, will incorporate the Bernier/Couillard affair into her act—the next time she comes to Canada.

Incidentally, the only thing Bernier leaves behind at Schwartz's is a tip, of the monetary—not of the dangers of politics —variety.

Rivers and her entourage split with the same fanfare as they had on their arrival. Night manager Mike Nelli comes up for a little air and reflects on life in the deli trenches. He notes, perhaps not so oddly, that the majority of the Schwartz staff has soured on smoked meat, though not on the deli itself.

Nelli also insists the best action takes place during his late shift. "That's when the stars and the wacky people come out," Nelli says. "That's when the politicians tend to show up, too."

Nelli was at the helm when former Prime Minister Paul Martin paid a surprise visit with his entourage of protectors. "He was very nice, but he also wanted me to give him a tour of the place," Nelli recalls. "So I took him from the entrance to the end of the restaurant and back. It is, maybe, about fifty feet long. He was a little stunned. He couldn't believe that's all there was to the famous Schwartz's."

Former Prime Minister Jean Chrétien didn't want a tour during his visit. Nor, for that matter, did Angelina Jolie, although Nelli professes he would have been only too willing to oblige.

"The wildest things that go on at night, though, tend not to involve famous people," Nelli explains. "How can I delicately put this? Well, there's been a lot of kinky stuff."

Evidently, one regular woman customer had a penchant for Schwartz's pickles and would delight in demonstrating uses other than oral for the veggie. "I don't blush easily, but she could do it all the time," Nelli says. "And the funny thing is the place was always packed at the time, and no one other than the staff noticed."

For the record, Nelli points out her pickle of choice was a half-sour. No gherkin for this gal.

Manny Pinaheiro has been cutting smoked meat for thirty-six years at Schwartz's. He's been around for all the owners, from Reuben Schwartz to Maurice Zbriger to Armande Chartrand to Hy Diamond. "Schwartz was the toughest," he says, careful not to bring his carving knife too close while wiping sweat from

Two night guys and a brisket. Cutter Manuel Pinheiro and counterman Paraounak (Bobby) Artinian.

his brow. "But otherwise nothing has changed here. It's still hot as hell behind the counter with all the steaming smoked meats."

Pinaheiro figures he's made as many sandwiches as an average McDonalds outlet has cranked out burgers: "Millions and millions. That's why I can't eat the meat any more."

Doug Whiteford, sitting at the counter in front of Pinaheiro, has taken a different route. He was a vegetarian before becoming smitten by Schwartz's smoked meat. "I just can't help myself from porking out on this stuff," he says.

Though he lives in Vancouver, Whiteford, a musician and composer, is yet another out-of-towner who makes Schwartz's his first stop in the city. "I've tried other stuff, like corned beef, when I'm in Vancouver. But it just doesn't cut it for me. I'm hooked on Schwartz's."

Whiteford wants to know how the pepperoni behind the counter tastes. Pepperoni?

No, no, he is told, that's karnatzel, a kind of Jewish sausage. "Then I must have it," he pronounces.

"That's remarkable. At this stage in my life, I've learned a new word: 'karrrrrr-natzzzzzzel.' Wow."

Astonishingly, Whiteford has even chowed down on spek. "Oh, you mean the fat and spice sandwich, it's great. But not every day. Really, I've only been disappointed here once—when I ordered a lean smoked meat. It wasn't memorable. But never again."

Something has caught Whiteford's attention. He appears startled. "What's that?" he points. "It can't be!"

Whiteford has just spotted a waiter, who will remain nameless, finishing off a container of yogurt. Schwartz's doesn't sell yogurt, or fruit, or any dessert, for that matter. Eating yogurt could be a hanging offense.

The same brazen waiter, after polishing off the yogurt, approaches Manny to ask if he would be more interested in ordering out for pizza or barbecue chicken. Manny isn't interested in any food. Whiteford, though, is alarmed. "Here they are sitting on the best grub in the world and they want to order out for pizza," says Whiteford. "It simply makes no sense at all."

Whiteford is now considering ordering a second sandwich. "I should have ordered the large plate of smoked meat, but I don't think I'm conditioned for that yet. I would pay the price. I'll have to build up my endurance. But on my next visit to the city I'll be ready."

Whiteford asks Manny about the bottled spices available for sale behind the counter. It's steak and chicken spice, Manny tells him. "I'll take both," Whiteford replies.

"Great," Manny shoots back. "Are they to eat here or to take out?"

Everyone's a comedian.

Meanwhile, manager Nelli would like to share memories other than those entailing different uses of half-sours. "One night a customer had a heart attack while eating," Nelli recalls. "But he was lucky. Sitting next to him happened to be a doctor. He gave him CPR and saved him. And wouldn't you know the guy was back the next week and still is a regular now."

The doctor?

"No, not him," Nelli says. "The heart-attack guy. Oh, yeah, there are lots of happy stories here, too. Like the time a customer started to choke, and I administered the Heimlich manoeuvre, and he spit out a chunk of smoked meat—but he was fine after that."

Cheque, please!

Waiter George Vidmar is another thirty year plus veteran.

Eight

Big Jean

IT's 11:20 IN THE MORNING. The sun is near blinding. But no matter how limited our vision, a familiar figure can be discerned loping up the Main. People on the sidewalk silently retreat to either side. It's like the parting of the Red Sea. Jean Béliveau is a little embarrassed. He does not wish to create a scene. He does not wish to draw attention unto himself. But he can't help it. More than forty years after he last donned the famed Habs sweater, Béliveau is still regarded as the ultimate hockey icon in this town. He embodies all that is great and gracious about the game of hockey in general, and the Montreal Canadiens in particular. He is a constant reminder of the Habs' glory years. As a player, he won and subsequently drank from the Stanley Cup ten times. As an executive and goodwill ambassador with Les Glorieux, he was part of another seven Stanley Cup winning teams.

Béliveau is a class act. Indeed, he is in a class all by himself. The last thing he is seeking this morning is to make a grand entrance. In fact, the reason he has arrived at Schwartz's this early is to avoid a line. Not that he would be averse to waiting and standing in line with regular folk for a seat inside, but he is fully aware that if any of the Schwartz's staff or, for that matter, his fellow standees in line see him, they will push him to the front of the line. And he abhors jumping lines almost as much as getting an errant elbow to the mug during his playing days.

"I can't help myself," softly says Béliveau, who is now sitting at an end table in the nearly deserted deli. "But when my wife and I have the urge for smoked meat, we come to Schwartz's.

We are almost magically drawn here. The smoked meat is the best, but it's also the atmosphere. It's a real people place. There is no pretentiousness here. Everyone is the same, and that's the way Élise and I like it."

"We've brought friends here from Scotland, France, Switzerland and even Barbados," adds Élise Béliveau. "They can't get over the place. They've never seen anything like it. And they can't get enough of the smoked meat. We have to send them out packages all the time.

Béliveau, still looking like a matinée idol at seventy-eight, has had a love affair with Schwartz's since he first made the permanent move here from the Quebec Aces in Quebec City and signed his first pro contract with the Habs in 1953. This is a marriage that has lasted as long as his own. But his penchant for smoked meat is not the reason he has been tagged Le Gros Bill. That predates his days both with the Canadiens and Schwartz's and goes back to his non-smoked-meat days with the Aces in the Quebec Senior Hockey League.

"They must be doing something right here," says Béliveau, a native of Trois-Rivières. "I don't think there is any other restaurant in the city that is eighty years old. There aren't too many businesses of any kind that have survived that long."

Apart from the Montreal Canadiens, that is.

"The success of the Canadiens is predicated on the fact that the team belongs to all the people in Montreal and, now, Quebec," Béliveau explains.

"And Schwartz's belongs to all the people of Montreal and Quebec," Elise interjects.

Of course, Béliveau points out, hockey has changed dramatically since he first laced up his skates at the old Forum in the early 1950s. "But nothing appears to have changed here. The grill looks the same. The smokehouse is the same. The tables and chairs seem the same. Even the employees' punch-clock looks the same," he says with a broad smile. "And, of course, the lineups outside are the same. That's why we make a point of coming here before 11:30 in the morning or after 11:30 at night, when it's a little less crowded."

"After we've been to shows at Place des Arts, we come here often," notes Élise. "It just makes us feel comfortable that when we come through the doors, everyone is an equal here—no matter if the person is bank president or on welfare. Or, yes, even a hockey player."

What even amazes Béliveau is the fact that Schwartz's hasn't franchised—like, say, the National Hockey League. Schwartz's owner Hy Diamond gives Beliveau the familiar refrain that he has been inundated with offers to franchise around the world, but has turned all comers down. He then explains the arduous and time-consuming process of making smoked meat the Schwartz's way, adding that there would no such quality control if Schwartz's ever franchised.

Finally, Diamond finishes with a variation of a favourite mantra: "There is only one Montreal Canadiens hockey team. And there is only one Schwartz's.

"We want to remain as unique to Montreal as Jean Béliveau is," Diamond states.

Béliveau nods. While a deli devotee of the first order, even Béliveau admits he couldn't have polished off a smoked-meat sandwich, dills, peppers and fries before a game. "That might not have worked so well," he says. "We would generally eat steak before a game in my day. Then I'd wait until after the game to come to Schwartz's."

"The amazing thing, though, is that it would melt in your mouth then and it still does today," says Élise.

What can't be as tasty for Béliveau and his bride is hearing stories of hockey players landing eight-figure contracts—for a single season. Béliveau, in spite of his heroics and Stanley Cups, had to settle for five-figure yearly salaries most of his career. His best contract came at the tail-end of his career, and it was for just a little more than $100,000 for a season. Today, that's well below the minimum wage for the most journeyman of players.

And yet Béliveau, who has been living in the same Longueuil home for well over fifty years, doesn't begrudge today's multi-millionaire players, even though they mostly pale in comparison to him. "What can I say? I was born thirty or forty years too early," he cracks, between mouthfuls of smoked meat. "But I had my time. I'm glad for these kids today. Still, they owe a tremendous debt of gratitude to Maurice (Richard), Gordie (Howe) and Bobby (Hull). And to the best player I ever saw, Bobby Orr. These players paved the way for this generation. And none of those guys earned the big money, either."

In 2005, Béliveau was the latest in a line of hockey stars from the pre-inflation period to auction off much of his memorabilia. The souvenirs generated close to a million dollars, which ensured that he and his family would have a little bit of a financial cushion. Béliveau's daughter, Hélène, and grand-daughters, Mylène and Magalie, had previously taken the pieces they wanted, like Béliveau's 500th goal puck.

Standing patiently over the table and listening to Béliveau is Catherine Kelly, clutching a placemat and pen in anticipation of an autograph. "I don't care how much money these players make today, not one of them has the class of a Jean Béliveau," she proclaims. "He's a true gentleman. The others could learn plenty from him."

"And many of these young players would jump to the front of the line," Élise quickly adds.

Meanwhile, Béliveau not only signs Kelly's Schwartz's placemat, but also poses for a picture with her. "This is one of the best days of my life," Kelly enthuses. "I'm in the company of two legends today, Jean Béliveau and Schwartz's. This is a double treat."

Like other fans, Kelly is struck by how well Béliveau has aged. "I was lucky," Béliveau explains. "I had only one really serious injury. I almost lost an eye. It was the first year of the curved blade and there were no limits then about how big the curve could be. Anyway, Stan Mikita (of the Chicago Black Hawks) nearly took out my eye with his blade. It wasn't intentional, but to this day my daughter Hélène still hates him for that.

"Otherwise, I was very fortunate. Apart from a broken cheek." Pause. "And a broken ankle and a few broken ribs. But really there wasn't much. Oh, I did sever a tendon a few times."

Béliveau is clearly not a complainer. Élise points out that he suffers from arthritis in his hands and has a dropped foot problem and that he did overcome a serious bout of cancer as well as a mild stroke. All of which explains why he hasn't been on skates for decades. "As I've gotten older, I've gotten a little lazier, so I don't work out as often."

There's lazy, and there's lazy. Few would accuse Béliveau today of being lazy. He still remains active with the Canadiens, showing up at every home game and greeting fans. He is also active with charity work that benefits disabled children. And few would have ever accused Béliveau of being lazy in his heyday with the Habs. Unlike today's stars, Béliveau needed a second job to pay the rent. Not long after he signed his first contract with the Canadiens, he also took a second job at Molson Brewery, where he was involved in everything from production to distribution, sales to marketing. And no matter how gruelling

Hy Diamond, Jean Béliveau and Bill Brownstein next to the usual line-up outside the restaurant.

a game he had the night before or a practice in the morning, Béliveau was expected to be at his desk every afternoon at Molson during the season and every day during the off-season. "That's just the way it was, but I was happy to have that extra income," says Béliveau, who left Molson after forty years in 1993 but still serves as the Habs' greatest-ever ambassador. "Hockey is my life. It's in my blood. It's made me who I am today. I have no complaints at all. The way I see it is that the glass is half full, not half empty."

It's that attitude that has earned Béliveau a place in the Hockey Hall of Fame, the National Order of Quebec, a Companion of the Order of Canada and a spot on Canada's Walk of Fame. No surprise to many that in 1994, Béliveau was asked to be Governor General of Canada, but he declined the offer. In 2001, he was paid homage with his portrait on a Canadian postage stamp.

Hovering over Béliveau now are Brian Orsato and his son, who wait, too, in the hopes that the former Hab will sign autographs and pose with them. "I was born in Montreal, but I live in Toronto now," Orsato says, before making this confession: "And I really, really hate the Leafs. I stay with the winners—like the Canadiens and, for that matter, Schwartz's. That's why I've brought my son here—to learn about his roots."

Béliveau obliges Orsato and his son with autographs, and then poses for pictures. "My father will die when I tell him I met you. He was your biggest fan back in the day. I just feel bad you didn't make the salaries these guys today do."

Béliveau simply smiles and says: "I wouldn't change any of it for a minute. Really, I am the luckiest man in the world."

Nine

Novice Counterman

THIS IS NOT A PROPITIOUS START. I need help tying up my Schwartz-issued apron in the back. Can't ask my old pal Stephen Phizicky, who just happens to have shown up for my first shift as a Schwartz's waiter. Purely coincidental, says a chortling Phiz. He's come in for lunch with Brian McKenna, his former CBC colleague and current partner on the independent TV production front in town.

I finally figure out how to tie a knot in the back without use of mirrors. Phizicky could care less. He says his tummy is grumbling. It's a fairly considerable tummy, too—although he says if I make reference to his girth there will be hell to pay down the road. Ah, but what's life without risk?

Phizicky orders a corner. In Schwartz's parlance, that's close to a quarter of a cow, smoked, steamed and top-heavy with fat and encrusted spices. McKenna opts for a ribber. That's a rib steak with all the trimmings, including a thumb-sized piece of hot dog and a small portion of liver.

Ribber, incidentally, is now accepted lingo. Decades ago, an old buddy, Art Fargeon, requested a ribber, and was served a liver steak. "That's not what I ordered," Farge protested. "That's what it sounded like," his waiter curtly replied. "I want a ribber," Farge shot back. "First, learn to talk properly," the waiter replied.

Times have apparently changed at Schwartz's. My boss for the day, Hy Diamond, says my job as a waiter is to service the customer. It's not the other way around as it was in those dark days, when waiters would take pride in insulting the customers, then chase them down the Main for not leaving a substantial enough tip. Gotcha.

McKenna recalls those days, when rude was da rage. He was dragged to Schwartz's for the first time back in 1967 by former *Montreal Star* writer Bruce Taylor. "Are you insane?" McKenna recalls telling Taylor. "The place is a dive." And not the place for good Irish lads to be seen in that era.

McKenna confesses his smoked-meat experience prior was similar to that of other goys. His mom would pop in these unappetizing-looking, frozen smoked-meat pouches into boiling water, and two minutes later her offspring was served something pink and rubbery and really, really wet between two slices of bread, likely white. McKenna, not surprisingly, wasn't impressed.

"Then I made the pilgrimage to Schwartz's with Taylor and I thought I had died and gone to heaven," he rhapsodizes. "It changed my life. I haven't stopped since. Of course, the waiters were so unbelievably rude."

McKenna apologizes for ordering the steak this time. He says it's a first. But he wants to try the liver entrée again. He recalls tasting Schwartz's liver the first time and remarking how it was totally unlike the liver and onions his mom used to force-feed him, sometimes at gunpoint.

Phizicky is frankly disappointing me. He has few insights to share. He grew up in this *quartier*. Word is that he opted for Schwartz's spek, not his mother's milk, as a tiny (relatively) tot. "I once smuggled in some Schwartz's into England while doing a shoot," he says. "And Mark Phillips (the former Montrealer who is a CBS-TV news correspondent) even brought some smoked meat into Moscow."

Thanks for sharing, Phiz. Is that the best you can do? "Just bring me my corner and shut up," the Phiz barks. "You're supposed to be working here, not haranguing the customers. I don't think I'm leaving you a tip."

The Irish guy, McKenna, has dozens of tales to recount. Interesting ones, too. During one of many events celebrating the life of late Montreal boulevardier Nick Auf der Maur, friends who were gathered at their favourite downtown watering hole, Ziggy's, had a sudden hankering for Schwartz's smoked meat. It was deemed that McKenna's daughter, Robin, would make the trek to Schwartz's to pick up sandwiches. An hour and a half later, she arrived back with the booty. The guys on hand were not amused. "What took you so long?" McKenna questioned his daughter. "Instead of taking a taxi, I walked back, to save a little money I could put in a fund for Nick," she replied meekly. Noble, perhaps, but one of the hungry, the late Mordecai Richler, went ballistic and mumbled something to the effect that a goy should never be entrusted to a task so serious as pro-curing smoked meat. McKenna reports, that after years of therapy, Robin appears to be getting over the trauma. Regard-less, she has never been asked to make the Schwartz's shlep again.

Attention next turns to this bizarre painting that hangs smack in the middle of the Schwartz's wall, surrounded by the rave reviews of the joint. The painting, depicting a gypsy musician from a bygone century, is clearly kitsch. Phizicky insists that I take it down.

Sorry, fellahs, would love to talk, but have to serve some other customers at the counter. An elderly couple have just sat down. They are drenched. It's teeming again outside. "I just had to have a sandwich," the gentleman says. "Me, too," says his wife. "We've come through hell and high water for this."

They're not just blowing smoke here. They have come through both. The Metropolitan Expressway sprung a leak and was flooded. The couple had come from Niagara Falls and had been headed to the Maritimes for a vacation. But they wanted to make a pit stop at Schwartz's. They must have had to paddle before negotiating a series of detours and rush-hour traffic to get to Schwartz's.

I clean the counter, take the order and inform the couple, Peter and Muriel Sokach, they could have made it to Moncton by now if they hadn't stopped. "It was beyond our control," says Muriel. "A higher power determined that we should stop here, so who are we to disagree?"

A few seats over, Tommy from Taiwan is snapping shots of Schwartz's between mouthfuls of his three medium-fat sandwiches. Tommy from Taiwan is a first-time customer, but he pledges he will be back with a gang the next time he's in town.

Next to him is Max, a local rock 'n roller. Max is a vegetarian. Has been for the last thirty years. But he falls off the wagon once a month for two lean. "Don't ask," he says. So I don't.

Meanwhile, I notice Jaime Gonzalez, who's working the counter with me, is starting to get antsy. "You serve this guy," Jaime says. No problemo. Then I take a look at the guy. He's about seventy, fit yet squat and really nasty looking. Think frenzied axe-murderer. He's from some indeterminate Slavic country. He's called Mr. Monday, because he has been showing up for thirty years every Monday afternoon at 4:30 p.m. Fine, except that this is a Wednesday afternoon. I'm getting a little creeped out.

"I vant a rib mit spices. Medium rare. You understand. If steak no good, I be mad," Mr. Monday informs me. He has this unsettling habit of pointing his steak knife in my face while talking. He looks familiar. That's right. *The Silence of the Lambs.* I'm sure he would be just as content dining on my liver as that of a cow.

"He's been scaring both staff and customers for the thirty years he's been coming here," says manager Frank Silva, who's joined me behind the counter.

Frank is so nervous he's eating a banana. Normally, the consumption of fruit or anything else that can be construed as healthy would be a firing offense. But there are exceptions. Mr. Monday, for starters.

No sooner do I figure out the prices and how to add a bill and then factor in taxes, Jaime figures I'm ready to learn the cash register. I balk. Too much input for one session, I tell him.

Mr. Monday is now trying to get my attention. I believe he's growling. I also believe that when he leaves the place he will be baying at the moon in the evening. Although not able to speak in tongues like Mr. Monday, I determine that he wants his bill. I'm nervous. My hands shake as I write and attempt to do the sort of long addition that was never my forte in school. Mr. Monday studies the bill and gives me a dark, menacing look. He disembarks his stool, still clutching his steak knife. Then he approaches the cash counter in front. He gets into an animated conversation with the cashier, all the while looking at me. He throws a few bills, yells something in Slavic or tongues in my direction and splits.

Jaime tries to relax me. Mr. Monday has left a 26-cent tip on his $22 bill. I'm not ready to retire just yet.

A couple of young women come to the counter. They're students from Virginia. One is at McGill, the other is visiting Montreal for the first time. The McGill student, in excellent French, orders a small plate of medium smoked meat. Her friend, in English, orders the same. They are very chatty and pleasant.

As I leave to get their order, I overhear the McGill student tell her friend: "That's why I love it here. The waiters are old-school pros."

Ah, an hour on the job, and my head is starting to swell like an old-school pro. Take that, Mr. Monday.

Next a couple from Kyoto, also first-timers, beam at me while they devour their sandwiches. Anything else, I ask. I hear "beer," when the young woman answers. I'm sorry we don't serve beer here. How 'bout black-cherry soda? No, she insists she wants beer. I'm sorry. After five minutes of back-and-forth banter, Jaime whispers in my ear that she doesn't want beer, just her bill. I'm sorry, I say. I give them their bill, and they bow. So I bow. Then they bow. And I bow. Jaime approaches me again to say I can stop any time.

I'm really getting into the swing of things now. A couple from New York City, also first-timers, hits the counter next. They order sandwiches and drinks. The girl, a real beauty, asks if it would be possible to have mayo instead of mustard on her sandwich. I am truly aghast. "Madame, mayo has no place at Schwartz's," I inform her with authority. "Why not?" she asks. "Because that would be wrong. It would be sacrilege and it would be disgusting," I reply with the same authority.

The two girls from Virginia are giggling. "You old-school waiters really know how to talk," the McGill student marvels.

Yes we do—although some of us inadvertently get our aprons tangled up in the pickle-fridge door.

The New York lady isn't finished, though. How 'bout some HP Sauce, she inquires. We have it, she is told, but that would be wrong and disgusting, too.

Jaime and Frank seem most entertained with my response. Owner Diamond decides it's time for a pep-talk: "Remember we are here to service the customer, not to scare them," he tells me, before adding, "Isn't it time you had a break?"

"OK, but only if you let me visit the fabled smokehouse in back. Diamond is distracted by a friend." So, mustering up all my courage, I sneak off into the kitchen and head for the smokehouse. I anticipate poisonous snakes and alien critters popping out of the foundation as I make the trek. I view my mission as something akin to that of Harrison Ford in *Raiders of the Lost Ark* as he tries to uncover the Holy Grail, the most sacred and mysterious treasure on Earth.

The smokehouse is adjacent to the kitchen. A cast-iron door, with a lock bigger than a brisket, keeps outsiders at bay. The lock is open and the door is slightly ajar. I open the door a little more. And there in all their splendour are dozens and dozens of smoked meats hanging on hooks. I've hit the mother lode. I half expect the voice of a deity to start speaking and to command me to remove myself immediately. But I am mesmerized by all the briskets, as one would be after tripping over a pot of gold.

Then a voice does sound. Why, it's Diamond. He tells me I'll reek of smoked meat for the next decade unless I extricate myself from the smokehouse. He also tells me I'm one of the fortunate few outsiders ever to witness this smoked-meat sanctuary and that I'm not to describe details of its construction to would-be smoked-meat mavens —14 cubits by 26 cubits by 17 cubits and much good shmutz—lest I face the wrath of the gods. Then the oracle that is Diamond speaks: "It's all in the bricks. That's the secret." And therein lies the shmutz.

"The new smokehouses they have today are made of metal," Diamond says, shaking his head. No need to finish the thought: metal doesn't store the shmutz.

I leave the smokehouse a more enlightened man. I feel like I'm almost floating. Manager Frank Silva shoots me a knowing glance. "You saw the smokehouse, eh? You must be one of the chosen."

Frank also tells me I might have a career as a counterman. He and the boys were talking, and they apparently agree that my voice was good. A counterman needs a voice that will rise over the din, one that the cutters will be able to make out clearly and never cause them to carve a lean when the order is for fat. "And you, my friend, have that kind of voice," Frank tells me. "You have a future here if you like."

I am humbled, and as I pass the counter, I holler, for no good reason, "one medium fat with no mayo." The cutters look up and smile. I've made it into a new fraternity.

Content on one level, yet unfulfilled on another. My quest for more knowledge must continue. I will not be able to sleep peacefully until I unravel the mystery and the enigma that is Reuben Schwartz. A deli god or a devil, inquiring minds must know. Or at the very least, this smoked-meat Magellan must know.

Bill with manager Frank Silva.

[Ten]

A Slice of Life?

PETER PENTELIS currently has the distinction of being the most veteran employee at Schwartz's. He began as a spry, ever-beaming twenty-year-old behind the broiler. And forty-five years later—and counting—he's still a spry, ever-beaming broilerman. In fact, it is believed that in the history of the place no one has surpassed this record. That's one hell of a lot of garlic he has sprinkled on his equally ageless grill.

Peter figures he's charbroiled untold thousands of rib and liver steaks during his tenure at temperatures hotter than Hades. When he started, he estimates he broiled about three hundred steaks a night. Eighty-five per cent of customers then opted for the grilled ribs and liver then. Today, he thinks it's the opposite with 85 percent of customers ordering smoked meat.

"Times change," he philosophizes. Not that he has anything against smoked meat. Au contraire. Peter claims he's in tip-top shape, and like lawyer Ed Blanshay, he attributes his excellent health to smoked meat. Curiously, he is among the few long or even short-term employees who professes a love for smoked meat. Most of the others, having pigged out on it for so long, now eschew smoked meat. "My attitude has always been that a sandwich or two a day keeps the doctor away," Peter croons. "I have never been to a doctor in my life, but they come to see me. They come to Schwartz's every day." Take that, Adelle Davis.

Apart from his daily dose of deli, Peter says his secret is sleep. Actually, sleep deprivation. He nods off only for three hours a night. "You snooze, you lose," he says, while flipping a couple of steaks.

Being another glass half-full kind of guy, he notes he has a permanent tan, without having had to spend major bucks going south to Florida or going a few blocks away from his home to a tanning parlour. His tan comes courtesy of the charcoal-burning grill.

If he ever does have to blow off steam, though, he'll simply chuck a few cold mini-franks, which, when grilled, garnish the Schwartz's rib and liver steak. Usually, Peter hits his intended targets, the waiters or smoked-meat cutters who may have accused him of not having changed his shirt for forty-five years. "Really, I'm just trying to wake the staff up. That's all. They are not always as alert as they should be."

But occasionally Peter misses his colleagues and hits an unsuspecting patron smack on the noggin. Rather than react negatively, the customer invariably triggers the Schwartz's equivalent to a food fight, with mini-franks flying everywhere. It's a tradition.

Peter also has had the distinction of working under every owner, from Reuben Schwartz to Hy Diamond. Ever the politician, though, he allows only that Schwartz could be demanding and that Diamond, standing a few feet away from him, is a gem. Upon further scrutiny, however, Peter insists Schwartz was decent to him, but could be very tough on other staffers. He also heaps praise on Maurice Zbriger who took over ownership after Reuben Schwartz. "Now there was class. He was No. 1," Peter says, within ear and eye shot of Diamond. "Just like Mr. Diamond, a class guy all the way."

And ever the politician, Peter plays no favourites among the politicians of different stripes he has grilled for over the years. "Pierre Trudeau, René Lévesque, Brian Mulroney, Jean

Peter Pentelis has been a broilerman since 1960.

Night manager Anthony Rowhani used to work next door at the landmark Warshaw's supermarket until it closed. In May 2006 he married Mary Maheu, Schwartz's night cashier.

Chrétien, Lucien Bouchard, Paul Martin—they've all come here. And they're all..." You guessed it: "class guys."

While Peter is reluctant to talk about his prowess behind the grill, not so his customers. Adam Benjamin, a trained chef, has eaten in the finest dining establishments in Montreal. At a moment's notice, he can cook up a feast with herbs and spices, veggies and fish that most Schwartz staff and customers have never heard of. But no foodie snob is he. He delights in bringing first-time visitors, chefs and regular folk alike, to Schwartz's for the fully-loaded rib steak at $14.95. "They are invariably blown away," Benjamin reports. "All the more so since they're accustomed to paying three and four times that price elsewhere."

Benjamin points out that during the Grand Prix here every June, the chichi Buona Notte, down the Main from Schwartz's, sells a 28-ounce steak for a walloping $180, and that Rosalie's and Queue de Cheval sell their 14-ounce sirloins for well over $60. And in the case of the latter steakhouse, the fries, baked potato and just about everything else are extra.

"Schwartz's gives you more bang for your steak buck than anywhere I know," says Benjamin, about to dig into a rib steak-smoked-meat combo. "It's important for people, especially chefs, to come to places like this to know what food really is. Man can't live on high-end alone."

Benjamin is equally delirious about the smoked meat. He marvels at the plate of meat, noting the way it is marbled. Then he approaches the plate and takes a whiff, before picking up his knife and fork to carve it up. "Gentlemen, start your Lipitor," he announces to his buddies at the table.

After a few mouthfuls, Benjamin, renowned for his use of truffles in the world of haute cuisine, comes up for air. "Some say smoked meat may be bad for you, but it tastes just so bloody good. Really, how could you not love salty meat with a lot of fat?" He's cracking a little wise here.

"The brisket isn't one of the choicer cuts of beef. It's a tough cut, which is why it has to soak up the spices here for nearly two weeks before being smoked for almost a day. The secret to Schwartz's success, I think, is in the brine they use to marinate. And because they turn over their meat so quickly, they don't have to inject it with nitrates or food dyes. There's no question Schwartz's has the best smoked meat in the city. The others are pretenders, some better than others, but mostly just taking up real estate."

This is all music to Schwartz's owner Hy Diamond's ears, or caretaker, as he likes to refer to himself. But he also attributes the quality of the meat to the gas-powered smokehouse at the rear of the restaurant. "That's where the flavour comes from," he says. "Spending at least seven hours in the smokehouse, and prior to that, spending at least ten days marinating in spices."

Diamond and Benjamin get into a conversation about how every brisket to come out of the smokehouse is different. "It's just like the great wines of Bordeaux," Diamond is so fond of saying. "Even if they bear the same label, not one tastes exactly the same as the next."

A customer, with a long face, approaches Diamond and whispers something in his ear. Diamond shakes his head and gives the customer a little hug. What gives? "The guy's son has... become a vegetarian," Diamond says with a shrug. "The man is in mourning. Four generations of the family had been coming here. Now he feels the cycle has been broken. He asked if there's anything I could do. I told him my own granddaughter is a vegetarian, but that hasn't stopped her from coming here and enjoying the cole slaw, pickles and fries. It's not such a tragedy."

Another of the philosophers gathered suggests that it might be time to think long-term, to come to grips with the ever-increasing number of health-conscious vegetarians. Montreal smoked "wheat" with a side of half-sour tofu. Mmmmm....

In fact, a local health-food entrepreneur has already come up with Montreal-styled smoked wheat which appears to incorporate the deli pickling process to a grain best known as a breakfast cereal.

Sheldon Chad, the TV writer, drops in again, now ready to expound upon his Monty Python/Schwartz's analogy. Chad grew up in the Snowdon district of Montreal, many kilometres to the west of the Main. He also grew up on Snowdon Deli, known for its smoked meat as well as its party sandwiches. Chad first discovered Schwartz's in the 1970s while attending nearby McGill University.

"I have to come clean here," Chad confesses. "I never found anything so special about Schwartz's."

A hush has come over the room. Diamond is initially taken aback, but soon starts to smile. "It's OK, son," he tells Chad. "You were young. You were impulsive. But you've come back to the fold."

Chad says his conversion came into effect only a few years ago. He had been living in Los Angeles for nearly twenty years, and it was upon his return that he came to fully appreciate Schwartz's.

"Maybe I was more mature. Maybe my tastes had changed. But I underwent an epiphany of sorts," Chad announces. He then proceeds to delve into the Python analogy. "I have to come clean again. When I first started watching Monty Python, I didn't get it. When I first came to Schwartz's, my taste buds didn't get it." Chad pauses for a sip of soda water. "Now I laugh like crazy at Monty Python. Now I can't get enough of Schwartz's. I've officially become a mensch."

There is much merriment in the room now. We don't know

whether to hoist Chad up on our shoulders and march him around the smokehouse or merely go out to rent Python's *Life of Brian* at the video store. Diamond is in a celebratory mood, and buys a round of smoked meat for the table. Good thing the place doesn't serve booze, or these impromptu celebrations could get out of hand and far more expensive.

"I have seen the light," Chad hollers. "There is only one bagel that matters in Montreal, and it comes from the St. Viateur Bagel Factory, and there is only one smoked meat that matters in Montreal, and it comes from Schwartz's."

Diamond looks like he's about to cry. Either that, or it's time for Tums.

"What can I say," Diamond responds. "I'm touched. Maybe it's the fact that we never have to refrigerate our smoked meat or pump it with chemicals and dyes." He repeats the process: the ten to fourteen-day marinating period, the seven hours in the smokehouse, and the one-and-a half hours in the steamer behind the counter. "And after all this, it takes about a minute for the smoked meat to disappear from the customer's plate."

"I had never entertained any notions of going into the restaurant business," Diamond confesses to Chad. "I had been Schwartz's accountant for a few years and then I bought the place in 1999. It was a huge gamble for me, but when does a mere mortal ever have the opportunity to become part of history?"

Diamond smiles and takes a long look around the place. "Go figure, this little hole in the wall is an icon in this country," he says. "When it opened on New Year's Eve in 1928, they would have locked Reuben Schwartz up if he had ever dared to suggest such a thing. Not in his wildest dreams could he have imagined such a thing. Who knew what that man dreamed of back then? It's a mystery to me."

[Eleven]

The Shadow

REUBEN SCHWARTZ was not a mystery to another Montreal legend. Yes, time has come to give the Shadow his due. OK, so the Shadow didn't smash the atom, but he has spiced up the lives of Montrealers like few others. Yup, apparently it was the Shadow who had the brain wave to garnish steaks with that special spice blend that is now a must at finer city chophouses.

It was back in the early 1950s when the Shadow, né Morris Sherman, was toiling as a broilerman at Schwartz's. The deal was that employees could eat whatever they wanted after work, just as long as it was liver. After a spell, the Shadow started to find his liver a little lifeless. So, he began sprinkling the spices used to flavour the smoked meat on his liver. And a legend was born.

Customers soon got wind of the smoked-meat spices on the liver and requested it. Then the Shadow had another inspiration: smatter those same spices on the rib steak. Sure enough, it was a hit at Schwartz's, and all the other steak joints in town followed suit.

For the record, sources also say it was the Shadow who prevailed on the management at Schwartz's to add the rib steak to the menu in the 1940s—'cuz the gut cannot survive on smoked meat alone and besides, business was a little slow at the time there anyway.

We're chewing the fat at the Main Deli, across the street from Schwartz's. The Shadow soon turns eighty. He's hung up his tongs after a noble career behind the broiler at an array of choice steakhouses in town. A triple cardiac bypass—perhaps the result of partaking of too much deli food—expedited his decision. But the Shadow still consults others in the biz about the rudiments of broiling and spicing. Turns out he has his Ph.D. in coleslaw preparation, too.

The Shadow allows me to sprinkle his secret spice on my steak. He waits for the smile he knows will soon come. But the Shadow is modest, not to mention stoic: "I was just a poor kid from the area who barely finished public school and did what I could to survive."

Oh yeah, they dubbed him the Shadow because he was so skinny as a kid that if he turned sideways in class the teacher would mark him absent. With his mane of silver curls, the Shadow—who now lives in Anjou, Quebec with his wife—is a fairly dashing fella, but he has put on a few pounds over the years. So just like the monicker Curly Joe stuck to the soon-to-be bald proprietor of that famed downtown steakhouse, the Shadow couldn't shake his nickname, either.

The Shadow was all of ten years old when he landed a waiter's job on weekends at Schwartz's. But his big break came four years later when Curly Joe handed him a smock and grill tongs and let him loose behind the broiler. It didn't take long for the Shadow to make it into the Pantheon of broilermen. He was in demand everywhere. At the height of his broiling prowess, the Shadow could grill fifteen steaks simultaneously on charcoal. He states there are a few keys to success. First, the steak must be well aged. Concentration is also a must—lesser broilermen would get easily distracted by adoring clientele peeping into the pit. But if a broilerman is to err, the Shadow insists one should err on the side of undercooking, because you can always bring the beef back for more sizzle.

So what about your secret blend of steak spice, Shadow? The Shadow deigns not to answer, merely flashing me the sort of perplexed look Colonel Sanders might have if someone had dared to ask him for his Kentucky Fried Chicken recipe. The Shadow does acknowledge, however, that the reward for being a brilliant broilerman was more on an artistic than a monetary level.

To that end, the Shadow had to be resourceful to keep himself amused when not broiling. But back in the early 1940s, when the country was at war and he was an adventurous teen, a dollar went a long way. A smoked-meat sandwich and soda at Schwartz's was thirteen cents. Three hours of movies and live entertainment at the Midway cost ten cents. "And a visit to the brothel around the corner only set me back fifty cents," the Shadow recalls. "Add the price of streetcar tickets to and fro for about six cents, and I still came home with money in my pocket. Ah, those were the days."

In 1946, though, the Shadow set his sights on more humanitarian concerns. With two cronies, he started the fabled Cartier Characters Association on the Main. "We got together mostly for laughs and then word spread and everyone wanted to join, so we charged them two dollars for membership and held elections for unofficial mayor," he says.

The Shadow opted not to run, paving the way instead for the irrepressible Ruby "Short-Butt" Brown, Max "Flop-Ears" Ziss and, of course, Red "The Goon" Fireball, who unsuccessfully attempted to install himself as unofficial Mayor for Life—clearly taking his cue from the political powers of the era. "I was just too busy in the pits to be the mayor," the Shadow sighs. "Look, I had to keep my cool over the coals."

But while the Shadow seems eager to discourse on spice and steaks and cronies of yore, he is initially at great pains to shmooze much about Reuben Schwartz. For good reason, his memories of the man are not laden with bliss. Yet few still breathing know more about the man than the Shadow.

"Reuben Schwartz was a miserable bastard," he barks over a cup of coffee.

Don't beat around the bush, Shadow, tell us how you really feel about the man. "OK, he was just one of the nastiest and cheapest people I have ever encountered in my life."

As mentioned, the Shadow was all of ten years old when he first started working for Schwartz back in 1930. Schwartz's had been open for a little more than a year, and being the Depression and all, business was not exactly booming. Consequently, Schwartz could hardly afford hiring seasoned waiters, so he took on school kids at far less than the lowest wages around.

The Shadow worked Saturdays and Sundays from three p.m. to midnight and earned all of fifty cents for his eighteen hours. That is, when he got paid at all. "Bad enough those were pitiful wages, but often he would just forget to pay me altogether," the Shadow recalls. "One time, he ended up owing me about five dollars and my father told me to march in and get him to pay me. I went in, and Schwartz just ignored me for the longest time. Then he said: 'Are you waiting to see me?'

"I told him I was. I also told that I would appreciate it if he could pay the five bucks he owed me. 'Are you threatening me?' he said. No, I told him I just want what was owing to me, that's all."

After an hour of wrangling, Schwartz eventually gave in, but left the Shadow with a taste more sour than the pickles. "Big surprise, with him running the place, it wasn't very popular," the Shadow says. "So when there were no customers to serve, he would make me peel potatoes, sweep the floors, clean the bathrooms and stock supplies in the back.

"Not only was he a miserable bastard, but he was also a bad

Morris "The Shadow" Sherman at eighty. At the height of his broiling prowess, The Shadow could simultaneously grill 15 steaks. This picture was taken across the street at the Main Deli where he was reminiscing with the Main's owner Peter Varvaro.

businessman. He went bankrupt twice, and had to be rescued by Maurice Zbriger, who not only bought the place from him but also let him live in his house because Schwartz couldn't afford to rent, much less buy, his own place. Small wonder he never got married, either."

The Shadow, normally a soft-spoken guy, is really getting worked up now. "It's unbelievable. He has one of the most famous names ever in this city, and the guy was just such a putz."

The Shadow now harks back to another painful memory from his youth. "My father decided I shouldn't work until midnight on Sundays at Schwartz's. He said I was only 10 and had to go to school the next day. So he said I should ask Schwartz if he could let me leave at 11:30 on Sunday night instead. No big deal we figured. So what does Schwartz tell me? He says I'd better be careful not to break a leg on my way home. Nice way to talk to a 10-year-old, eh?"

After a few years, the Shadow could no longer take it. So he quit. "Schwartz was furious at me for leaving. Things were so bad there that the guy who cut the smoked meat had to serve it, then clean up. All he could afford was that guy, someone in the kitchen to make fries, and me and another kid."

For reasons the Shadow and many others could never figure out, Schwartz was befriended by musician and composer Maurice Zbriger and his wife Mary, who took him in when he was at the end of his financial rope. "People used to joke that while Zbriger was making music upstairs in his home, Schwartz was making music to Mary downstairs. Nice guy, eh?"

The Shadow did return to Schwartz's years later as a broiler-man/waiter. "The only reason I returned is that Zbriger, who was much more into his music than his meat, was really running the show, with Schwartz acting as his frontman. Then I was making the princely sum of $16 a week plus tips."

Fronting or not for Zbriger, Schwartz, according to the Shadow, started to pocket six dollars from his sixteen as a sort of commission. So the Shadow bolted Schwartz's again. "I just couldn't figure that guy out. He was a tall, good-looking man. He was in decent shape. Yet he never, ever smiled. He liked to hire kids or new immigrants he could take advantage of."

The Shadow would invariably run into Schwartz on the Main over the years. "I would keep my distance and not say anything. But he would delight in telling whoever he was with how he used to feed me as a kid and take care of me, but now I had become his sworn enemy. He had a short memory of how he treated me and the other employees."

According to the Shadow, Schwartz had a brother in Paris and another in Toronto. "The Toronto brother even came to work with him at Schwartz's, but, big surprise, discovered that like nearly everyone else he couldn't get along with him," the Shadow says.

No matter how much he despised the man, the Shadow does give Reuben Schwartz his due as a true smoked-meat pioneer. "Sure he had to borrow money from local butchers to stay afloat and keep one step faster from his creditors, but he made a hell of a smoked meat. He had his secret recipe of spices he brought over with him from Romania. The key was that he let the briskets marinate for nearly two weeks and he never used any preservatives or dyes like the other delis did. No nitrates to make the meat red, either. And today they still follow the same system."

The Shadow acknowledges there was a change in Schwartz's fortunes around the time Montreal hosted Expo 67. Travel and restaurant writers from around the world got wind of this quaint, old-fashioned deli and word soon spread like wildfire.

Suddenly, tourists from the U.S., Europe, the Middle East and Asia started to outnumber locals for the sixty-one spaces at the restaurant.

The Shadow could see there was gold in that smoked meat. When Reuben Schwartz died in 1971, the Shadow paid a visit to the deli and approached Maurice Zbriger with an offer to buy the place. "I told him I'd give him $15,000 immediately and more to follow. Zbriger, though he wasn't much interested in being a deli owner, told me he had just turned down $500,000 for the place, but thanked me all the same."

To get back at Reuben Schwartz, the Shadow gave what he presumed to be the Schwartz smoked-meat recipe to his buddy Peter Varvaro, owner of the Main Deli. But a recipe is only good if you have the old-fashioned Schwartz's smokehouse, which the Main and the others don't. They have newer metal varieties, and the Shadow acknowledges, that as a consequence, the Main and the others have not been able to replicate Schwartz's smoked meat. "You can know which spices to sprinkle, but the trick is to know how much to sprinkle."

The Shadow recalls bringing down smoked meat to his sister in New York. She, in turn, brought it over to the local deli. "The guy there tried it and said it was different, but you could tell he wasn't really impressed. I told the guy I had the spices and that if he wanted to follow the formula, he could make Montreal-styled smoked meat. I told him he'd have to marinate the brisket for at least 10 days. He looked at me like I was nuts."

The Shadow seems to have answered one of life's conundrums in the process. He discovered that most American delis only pickle their meat for around five days. "They also punch holes in the brisket to expedite the process. They then put the meat in this modern metallic smokehouse, but it comes out all dry and flavourless by my standards. Then they leave it in a steamer for far too long, in order that it doesn't shrink.'

The Shadow believes he could have made the New York deli dude rich, but he just wouldn't bite.

"All the same, I never in my wildest dreams could have ever imagined that Schwartz's would be what it is today," the Shadow says. "Not with a Reuben Schwartz as the boss, anyway. All I can recall are incidents like the time he came into the restaurant when there was just me. No customers at all. He caught me reading a newspaper. He yanked it away from me and screamed: 'This is not a library, kid!'

"Even when business picked up for him, he had no natural instincts. Customers would ask why he didn't buy the place next door when it went up for sale. He would tell them that he'd rather have a small place that was always full than a big place that was half-empty."

Then again, the Shadow concedes that Schwartz may have been on to something. From our vantage point at the larger Main Deli across the street, we can see large lineups outside Schwartz's and it's almost nine p.m. The Main, which does divine rib steaks comparable to Schwartz's, is half-full—empty?

Mike Sawiries, the Main broilerman, spots the long lineup outside Schwartz's, too. "What's the secret?" he asks, then briefly answers. "Everyone now seems to have Schwartz's branded in their brains. Without spending anything on advertising, they've managed to make everyone here and just about everywhere else think that Schwartz's and smoked meat are synonymous." He pauses to wipe his brow. "Of course, it doesn't hurt that their smoked meat is always fresh, because they have so much turnover."

Kind of like the chicken and egg theory, suggests Sawiries.

A lightbulb appears to have suddenly turned on in the Shadow's mind. "There was something really odd and funny about Reuben Schwartz. Over all the years I worked for him and visited the place, I never, ever once saw him eating smoked meat. The father of smoked meat, and he didn't touch the stuff. Strange, eh?"

And then again, perhaps not.

Maurice Zbriger, Reuben Schwartz, Montreal police officer Richardson, and Schwartz's accountant (name unknown), circa 1960. This may be the only known photograph of founder Reuben Schwartz.

[Twelve]

The Zbriger Legacy

IF REUBEN SCHWARTZ, who died in 1971, was an enigma, so, too, was his successor at the deli, Maurice Zbriger. Yet while Schwartz was a man of mystery with precious few details available about his background, his family or his interests, Zbriger's life was, by comparison, an open book. That is, the parts of that book he wished to share with the public.

A few weeks after he passed away in 1981 at the age of eighty-four, a lengthy obituary with a photo of Zbriger appeared in the Montreal *Gazette*. "Montreal music circles recently lost a revered and highly esteemed member with the death of Maurice Zbriger, well-known violinist, composer and conductor," the obit began.

It then went on to chronicle Zbriger's life, noting that he was born in the Ukraine and that at the age of twelve, he was accepted at the Russian State Conservatory in Leningrad. He was a pupil of Leopold Auer and among his classmates were the later-to-become legendary Jascha Heifetz, Nathan Milstein and Mischa Elman. When he later moved to Moscow, he was a member of both the Symphony Orchestra and the Operatic Orchestra there.

It was then revealed that with his wife Mary, who pre-deceased him, he toured the concert halls of Europe before arriving in Montreal in 1924. Once ensconced in the city, Zbriger was a member of the orchestra at His Majesty's Theatre, as well as those of the Capitol and Palace Theatres, where the musicians would provide accompaniment to the silent films of the era.

Zbriger became first violinist in the Montreal Symphony Orchestra in 1930, before forming his own band, Maurice Zbriger and his Gypsy Ensemble, which performed regularly for more than four decades on radio at CFCF, CKAC and CBC.

The obit also mentioned that he and his wife continued composing and later set up the Maurice and Mary Zbriger Concerts, which offered Montrealers free international music for twenty years, first at Plateau Hall, then at Man and His World and finally at Place-des-Arts.

Zbriger counted among his closest friends Paul-Émile Cardinal Léger and Mayor Jean Drapeau, for whom he signed the Golden Book at Montreal City Hall.

Astonishingly, what was never even alluded to in this obituary was that Zbriger was the owner of Schwartz's at the time of his death. What makes this omission even more startling is that it was his smoked-meat money that enabled Zbriger to live fairly lavishly, to compose, to hire musicians, to rent the best halls in the city and then to give away thousands of tickets for free.

Although their history is murky at best, it is known that Zbriger became friends with Reuben Schwartz in the 1930s, that he took in Schwartz to live at his home after the latter suffered few financial reversals years later, that he became a silent partner in Schwartz's in the late 1950s, and that he became sole proprietor of the deli following the death of Reuben Schwartz in 1971.

By all accounts a genial boss and a gracious man, Zbriger clearly did not want to be recognized for his contributions to the world of deli.

Even in an extensive interview with Eleanor Callaghan in the Montreal *Star* four years before his death, Zbriger shared many of the most intimate details of his life, save for his involvement in Schwartz's. "I sometimes think I have the soul of a

Maurice Zbriger married his wife Mary in 1915 when he was nineteen.

gypsy," he recounted. "As a very small boy, I stood around watching and listening to fiddlers playing at village weddings and parties. When I was about five, my grandmother gave me twenty cents to buy nuts. Instead I got a toy violin and a little while after got my first real one. There were no musicians in my family. My father was a poor man and couldn't afford to give me lessons."

Callaghan also unearthed the facts that Zbriger married Mary when he was but nineteen in 1915 and that the newlyweds had to bolt the country with the onset of the Russian Revolution a few years later. They played for Europe's café society before deciding to immigrate to the U.S. But because of a death in the family, they missed their opportunity to move there and had to console themselves with Canada.

However, it wasn't a propitious start in the New World. When his ship first docked in New York on its way to Montreal, Zbriger was arrested. "The immigration people thought I was a Bolshevik," he told Callaghan. "I was kept at Ellis Island (New York's immigration detention centre) for two weeks and then sent over the border to Montreal accompanied by a detective."

Zbriger allowed that it wasn't initially easy, all the more so since he didn't speak much English, but that he and Mary did

A young Maurice Zbriger before he came to Canada.

love Montreal "from the first minute." After he learned to play "O Canada"—which he had never heard before—musical opportunities evidently beckoned.

Montreal *Star* readers further learned that Zbriger had an electric elevator in his home, that arthritis eventually curbed his violin playing and that he owned a 1776 violin made by a student of Stradivarius. But not even a speck about spek or smoked meat or liver or rib steaks or Schwartz's.

Far more about this enigma was to be uncovered in the National Film Board of Canada documentary *The Concert Man*, which followed Zbriger during his final years but which came out after his death. Directed by Tony Ianzelo, with a narration written by William Weintraub, this film establishes Zbriger as a violinist, a dreamer and a romantic figure who always attracted women. It also confirmed that while Zbriger studied at the conservatory in Leningrad with Heifetz and Milstein, he never reached the same musical heights as the latter.

And, oh yes, the documentary does acknowledge in no uncertain terms that Zbriger was very much the deli entrepreneur who took over Schwartz's and, moreover, that smoked-meat monies allowed him to pursue his dreams. Yet, when Zbriger sauntered into Schwartz's with his wife, he would always act like a customer, not the owner.

Jack Lieber, an acquaintance and former English professor who appears in the film, notes that Zbriger wanted to be known for his music, not his smoked meat. "He felt the restaurant business to be demeaning," explains Lieber. "I was sworn to secrecy the first time that I met him not to speak publicly about his role as owner of Schwartz's."

There is a scene nothing short of surreal in the NFB documentary. It captures Zbriger, Mary and an entourage of classical music buffs, all dressed to the nines, marching into Schwartz's.

They take a back table and, over imported cake, burst out singing a selection of arias. They are as oblivious to the customers inhaling their smoked-meat sandwiches as the customers are oblivious to them.

One of the more interesting details to emerge from the documentary is that Zbriger's bride Mary came from a wealthy family and that he managed to smuggle out her sizable dowry from Russia in his violin case—perhaps his grandest bit of fiddling in retrospect. It was this dowry that later enabled Zbriger to purchase Schwartz's and that proved to be the best investment he had ever made—no matter how reluctant a deli entrepreneur he was.

Zbriger was so devoted to Mary that when she became ill he took care of her and ceased trying to establish himself as a world-class violinist. But it didn't prevent Zbriger from composing classical compositions for world figures, including royalty, popes and millionaires. Lieber, the prof, would then pen letters for Zbriger to these people, explaining how Zbriger had written these pieces in their honour. For good measure, he would sometimes even pack Schwartz's smoked meat along with the missive. "He just had this lifelong obsession about being recognized for his music," Lieber says.

It turns out, though, that Zbriger's claim of being close buddies to Paul-Émile Cardinal Léger was accurate. In the film, Léger is seen visiting Mary Zbriger during her final days in a hospital. Though Jewish, Zbriger reveals to Léger and others that he owes the Catholic Church a huge debt of gratitude for helping to nurture his musical dreams.

Another piece of the Schwartz's puzzle falls into place in the documentary. An attractive woman by the name of Armande Toupin gradually plays a larger and larger role in Maurice Zbriger's life. After the passing of Mary, the task of catering to

Leger visits sick friend

Cardinal Leger yesterday had a chit-chat with an old friend . . . he and celebrated Montreal composers and musicians Mary and Maurice Zbriger, both over 80, have been friends for 25 years. Mary is in satisfactor condition at the Royal Victoria Hospital after being ad mitted for what a friend said was routine testing

Cardinal Léger visited Mary Zbriger in the hospital before she died.
Montreal *Gazette* clipping, 1980.

Zbriger's needs is largely left to Toupin. She dotes over him. She cooks and chauffeurs him. She cleans his home. More importantly, she becomes the guiding force behind Zbriger's free concert series at Place-des-Arts. She coordinates the music selections, hires the musicians, rents the hall and writes the cheques.

But Toupin's yeoman efforts were not to go unappreciated by Zbriger. When he passed away, he left the extremely cultivated, world-travelled Armande Toupin Chartrand (as she was known after she married) a small gift—Schwartz's. Armande, quite the gourmand, knew plenty from smoked oysters and foie gras, but next to nothing from smoked meat and spiced liver steaks.

Meanwhile, years later, Lieber and his buddy, William Weintraub, still remain baffled by Zbriger. "He was the most pretentious man imaginable," says Weintraub, author of the bestselling probe into Montreal's Sin City days, *City Unique*. "Yet, oddly, there was nothing dislikable about his pretensions."

Lieber became so consumed with Zbriger that he has undertaken a biography on the man. He and Zbriger were introduced by one Bert Greenford, "a depressive melancholic who would periodically plop himself down in my living room, bitch about the unfairness of life, dissolve into tears, then disappear into the night."

One night, Greenford was griping to Lieber about his problems penning letters for a "wealthy, barely literate eccentric, the Russian-Jewish proprietor of a delicatessen on the Main." Greenford asked Lieber if he would be willing to undertake the job. Lieber agreed and a meeting was arranged.

"Zbriger's arrival into our living room was presaged by a nimbus of powerful cologne and a glitter of gold cufflinks and diamond rings," Lieber remembers. "His hair was pomaded over a balding pate and cunningly arranged to blanket as much as possible of the exposed surface. A fixed smile revealed a magnificent set of dentures unmatched in their luminescent regularity."

Lieber soon learned what his assignment would be. He was to write letters of dedication to important people that would accompany musical manuscripts of Zbriger's compositions. Zbriger then produced previously-written letters with their accompanying compositions: "The Canadian National Railways March" dedicated to Sir Henry W. Thornton, president of the CNR; "The Canadian Pacific Railway Waltz" dedicated to the boss of that railway; "The Lord Nuffield March" dedicated to Lord Nuffield of Mini Minor fame; and "Moonglow Romance" dedicated to Astor Sweets, a Montreal bistro that once employed Zbriger the gypsy violinist. What the compositions had in common was a schmaltz-like quality. "When Zbriger showed me the scores of these musical compositions, it was difficult to

Maurice Zbriger composed the Lord Nuffield March in honour of industrialist William Morris—Lord Nuffield—founder of Morris Motors.

Sheet music for *The Little Cuckoo* composed by Maurice Zbriger.
Published by Popular Music Publishing Ltd., 1928.

keep a straight face, but I need not have worried. His incredible self-preoccupation and childlike naïveté bred a humorlessness that could never be penetrated. Nor was he aware of the chintzy tenor of his compositions, although to be fair they were no worse in their musical platitudes than the Sousa/Strauss models he chose to emulate."

Throughout all their encounters over the years, Zbriger not only kept his ownership of Schwartz's a secret, but also his wife Mary. She was another enigma, whose role, it seemed, mostly revolved around boosting her husband's ego as a musician.

Despite his impressive resumé, Lieber doesn't beat about the bush assessing Zbriger's skills in the fiddling department. "He was absolutely terrible. The hardest thing in the world for me to do was to keep a straight face while he played."

Perhaps then he was more adept at composing. Not bloody likely, according to Lieber. "He was an uprooted gypsy violinist of limited talent who composed pseudo-Sousa shlock," Lieber states. "What Zbriger wanted more than anything was to bond with the rich and famous."

So to that end, Lieber wrote the most flowery letters possible to the rich and famous. Lieber, attending university back then and in dire need of cash, earned the princely sum of fifty dollars a letter. And he sent them out by the score to everyone from Pope John XXIII, Queen Elizabeth, the Canadian Governors-General Massey and Vanier, Cardinal Léger, Jacqueline Kennedy Onassis, Margaret Truman and, for some bizarre reason, British auto magnate Lord Nuffield.

To wit: Zbriger's December 1, 1960 letter to the Pope:

Your Holiness,
    I humbly beg Your Holiness's indulgence to address you. The very act of writing to you fills me with a sincere

awareness of my own insignificance. Yet I know Your Holiness's Supreme understanding and love for all men is such that my letter to you will be taken in the humble spirit with which it is written ... My own humble contribution to you is music, for this is my whole life. I am by faith a Jew, by trade a violinist and composer of music, by conviction a man of peace. I beg leave therefore that you look upon my offering to you as a small and insignificant token of my religious feelings. This token consists of two compositions of mine, an 'Ave Maria' and 'Notre Père,' both in manuscript form, together with a recording of these compositions....

Your Devout Servant,
Maurice Zbriger

Lieber doesn't recall if he packed any smoked meat with this missive as he often did with most of the others. But he does recall that "I was always shitting my pants, laughing hysterically writing these letters." He also recalls Zbriger's joy when his letters were answered. "If he received something back from the Pope or Governor General, he was absolutely euphoric. He was where he wanted to be. This was his raison d'être. Sometimes these letters even got him invited to garden parties in Ottawa." However, these parties also proved problematic. Lieber had to instruct Zbriger what to wear and, on more than one occasion, had to remind him to zip up his fly.

Lieber does acknowledge that he was handsomely rewarded for his letter-writing. In addition to the cash, Lieber received musical instruments, clothing for his family and, natch, all the smoked meat he ever desired. With much pomp and circumstance Zbriger would invariably show up at Lieber's digs with a chauffeur bearing gifts and deli. Zbriger would pull out a jar of

Little Bells are Tinkling composed by Maurice Zbriger.
The inscription reads: "To my dear friends Mary [Jack's first wife] & Jack
Lieber with all my best wishes."

Maurice Zbriger (centre) was honored at a testimonial dinner last night for his contribution to Montreal music.

With him are Wally Newman (trumpet) and Joe Miceli (saxophone).

(Gazette, George Cree)

A high note for Maurice...

Maurice Zbriger, a gypsy violinist and composer who has been playing on Montreal radio stations from more than 40 years, was honored last night at a testimonial dinner given by the Musicians' Guild of Montreal.

Zbriger started his musical career in Leningrad, U.S.S.R., at the age of twelve as a pupil of the well-known teacher Leopold Auer.

In his class were Jascha Heifetz and Nathan Milstein, both now world renowned violinists.

"I retired twenty years ago," said Zbriger. "but I've never stopped playing and composing. Music is my life, and if I stopped making music, I would die."

Zbriger has written 250 pieces of music in his life,

and has received many awards, including a medal from the France Brittanique Society of Paris.

He now conducts free concerts of his own compositions in Lafontaine Park and Plateau Hall in Montreal.

Zbriger is the owner of the Montreal Free Hebrew Delicatessen, also known as Schwartz's Delicaten.

Maurice Zbriger honoured at testimonial.
"Music is my life, and if I stopped making music, I would die."
Montreal *Gazette* clipping.

118

Maurice Zbriger attended Iris and Jack Lieber's wedding
in Montreal, April 1, 1961.

kosher pickles and tomatoes and present it to Lieber and his
bride as if it were gold. "Then digging deep into another bag,
Zbriger conjured forth a clutch of sandwiches each cocooned
in its chrysalis of oiled paper so that not a smidgen, not a drop
of brisket dripping could escape; each sandwich a quivering
blush of tongue-shaped slices of spiced smoked meat; each slice
rimmed with a golden ribbon of peppered fat and everything
snuggled into the embrace of crusty rye bread slathered with
lashings of mustard."

Clearly, Lieber was a fan. Yet, curiously, in the thirty years
he knew the man, Lieber never once saw Zbriger chomping on
a smoked-meat sandwich. Some suspect that Zbriger, who considered himself to have hailed from noble Russian stock, may
have been embarrassed about the Romanian roots of smoked meat.

In 1982, the NFB's film, *The Concert Man*, celebrated the life of Maurice Zbriger, the enigmatic violinist, composer and delicatessen owner.

Not so coincidentally, during Zbriger's reign at Schwartz's, a couple of jokes constantly made the rounds:

"What's the difference between a Romanian and a Polack? Both would sell their mothers, but the Romanian would also deliver." Or this ditty: "How do you make a Romanian omelet? First, you steal the chicken..."

Lieber has another theory. He often wondered why Zbriger didn't eat smoked meat or anything else in his company. "He was more content to play a voyeuristic role. It was only later I learned that he was an obsessive-compulsive, not only about the food he ate but also the plates on which it was served. This was one of several neurotic syndromes that coloured his behaviour. Even the bank notes with which he paid me for the letters had to be newly minted and fresh from the bank. He said he didn't like other people's used possessions in his pocket."

Yet here's the kicker: Lieber may not have been blown away by the man's eccentricities or musical talent, but he was thoroughly impressed with Zbriger's deli-management prowess. "He never wanted to be thought of in this vein, but he was an absolutely fabulous businessman. He turned Schwartz's around and is largely responsible for turning into the success it has now become."

Nevertheless, Lieber has come to believe there is much murkiness left unanswered in the relationship between Reuben Schwartz and Maurice Zbriger. "My own suspicion is that there was an unsavoury bond between the two of them. I don't know the reason. The two wouldn't seem to have had much in common on the surface. That's why Zbriger always tried to keep his distance from Schwartz's. And yet Zbriger made an absolute fortune from Schwartz's. He was also incredibly generous and was a benefactor to musicians and artists. His greatest moments came when he waved his baton at his concerts at Place-des-

Arts. But he was really just a marionette. A real conductor was leading the orchestra behind the scenes. Still it was Zbriger who received the ovations from his friends in the audience. He lapped it all up. He lived to be adulated. But only for his music."

And there's the rub. The music is long forgotten, even the "Lord Nuffield March." But the smoked meat lives on like some classic piece of art, loaded with the sort of shmaltz people actually covet. And thanks to Zbriger, the legacy of Schwartz's also lives on, which is probably cold comfort to him in his final resting place.

Maurice Zbriger (second from the right) and his band
of merry men.

Thirteen

La Grande Dame

IT'S A GLORIOUS SPRING DAY. We're having a late lunch at a primo ringside table at Le Paris, the venerable downtown Montreal bistro that offers patrons a pulse of the city without ever having to leave their seats. We're sipping champagne, the favourite libation of Armande Toupin Chartrand, but we're talking about love and, seemingly incongruously, smoked meat.

Chartrand has clearly aged since her days organizing the minutiae of Maurice Zbriger's life almost three decades back. But once a grande dame, always a grande dame. Perfectly coiffed and made up, decked out in her finest French designer garb, Chartrand has the Le Paris staff jumping at her every request. "Ze champagne, not chilled enough to your satisfaction, Madame?" the waiter asks, before quickly responding: "No problem, Madame, we put more ice in ze bucket. Yes?" Madame simply nods.

Tourists at an adjacent table would have every reason to suspect that Madame is some kind of royalty. And in a way she is. Chartrand has earned her place in the Pantheon of Montreal icons, as owner of Schwartz's for nearly twenty years. Ironic, too, since the Paris-born-and-finished Chartrand would seem a far more likely candidate in the fashion or arts hall of fame in France. Also seated at the table is Hy Diamond, the current owner who purchased the deli from Chartrand in 1999. He fits the role of deli baron far better.

Chartrand, delicately clutching her goblet of champers in

Armande Toupin Chartrand circa 1981. She was the Zbrigers' loyal friend, and acted as Maurice's impresario. According to lore, she liked to have her friends in at Schwartz's for high tea in the late afternoon and insisted that her deli table be covered with a checkered tablecloth.

one hand, seems a little lost in reverie. She gazes through the window and appears to be focusing on the abundant human traffic swarming along Ste. Catherine Street. Rites of Spring in Montreal invariably entail the shedding of cumbersome winter wear and the donning of revealing summer wear—even if there is still an Arctic bite in the air—by the city's unending legions of spectacularly attractive women. "Nowhere in the world are the women as gorgeous," Chartrand notes. "And the men aren't so bad, either." She giggles. She is not far wrong, either—in her assessment of the city's women anyway. Indeed, the city's women and smoked meat could be in a dead heat in terms of Montreal's most renowned—natural?—resources. Yet it's also a fair bet that few of the pulchritudinous masses indulge at Schwartz's regularly. Madame, on the other hand, has no such qualms. She could just as easily feast on *viande fumée*—the literal French translation for smoked meat that is almost never used by Montrealers who tend to call it smoked meat. "I lovvvvve deli," Madame gushes. "Even hot dogs." Madame is one of the few people on the planet who can make hot dogs sound sexy.

However, since Le Paris has no smoked meat or hot dogs to offer, Chartrand opts for the pâté and fiddleheads to start, poached salmon (sauce on the side, please) and, why not, some frites, too. Diamond and I follow her lead. Not that we have much choice. Madame has ordered for us, because Madame knows what's best for us.

During her tenure as Queen of Schwartz's, Chartrand had a couple of endearing quirks. According to lore, she liked to have her friends in for high tea in the late afternoon and insisted that her deli table be covered with a checkered tablecloth. No one recalls if cucumber sandwiches on crustless white bread were served, but there were dainty pastries imported for the occasion. Much like Zbriger and his opera-loving cronies who remained oblivious to the Schwartz's clientele, and vice versa, Madame and her entourage carried on like they were at the Ritz.

"It's all about love," Madame rhapsodizes. She's not referring to the couple groping on the other side of the restaurant window. "The story of Schwartz's has almost nothing to do with business. Love brought us all together, and the place prospered in spite of itself. Of all the owners, only Hy (Diamond) has any business background, so it's not surprising that Schwartz's is now far more successful than it has ever been."

Madame weaves a most mystifying, yet intriguing, tale of romance that has been the hallmark of Schwartz's since its inception. She, too, does not dispute the notion that founder Reuben Schwartz was a difficult and demanding man. "He never married," she says. "Not even his brother Morris, who once worked the broiler at Schwartz's, could work with him. Even when women made the effort, like Schwartz's Rita (Samchuck), he managed to alienate most people."

Somehow, though, Maurice and Mary Zbriger saw something in Reuben Schwartz. "When business failed, when his money dried up, they were not only at the ready but they took him into their home to live," Chartrand says. "They learned to love a man no one else seemed to love. Mary was especially kind to him, while Maurice was always there for him, no matter what the crisis. This was truly a love story."

The love story continued with the passing of Reuben Schwartz and Mary Zbriger. When an elderly Maurice Zbriger was afflicted with worsening arthritis, Chartrand (then Toupin), a big fan of Zbriger's music and concert series, took it upon herself to care for the man. All were in awe as Chartrand made sure that every facet of Zbriger's life was under control. Even prior to Mary's passing, it was Chartrand who would drive her

Program for the Zbriger concert dedicated to the Musicians'
Guild of Montreal, Place-des-Arts, October 22, 1979.

to doctors appointments and spend time with her at the hospital. Then she would head back to the couple's home to clean it, do the laundry and prepare meals.

Chartrand took on even more with Maurice Zbriger. In addition to taking care of household chores, she also served as an impresario of sorts, overseeing his concerts. She selected the music, hired the musicians, rented the concert hall and distributed the tickets. No easy task.

"I never thought about doing this for any future rewards," Chartrand says. "I was simply motivated by my love for Mary and Maurice and for the music. Someone had to do it. Otherwise, the music would have died. But in none of my fantasies growing up did I ever think that one day I would own the most famous smoked-meat restaurant in Montreal, maybe the world."

She smiles. "But that's what I mean. Schwartz's was never about business. It was a love affair, and that love affair continues today."

In the pay-it-forward scheme of things, Diamond now ensures that Chartrand, a widow, gets to her medical appointments on time. In fact, when not at his regular table at Schwartz's, it's a good bet he's chauffeuring Chartrand around town. "What's most remarkable is that the main thing that has bonded the owners of Schwartz's, since Reuben Schwartz, has been compassion," she explains. "I know that Hy will always be there for me, as I was for Maurice, as Maurice was for Reuben.

"Life has just taken so many strange turns, but who could ask for a more interesting life? Who could have ever known that a young schoolgirl from Paris would have ended up like this? But I'm grateful for it all. Besides had I never ended up in Montreal, I would have been denied one of life's great pleasures: gefilte fish."

[Fourteen]

From Boston to Burundi, It's a Hit!

IT WAS ALMOST 20 YEARS AGO that Boston film critic and writer
Gerald Peary came to Montreal in search of movie gems at the
Montreal World Film Festival. Peary believes he actually did
uncover the occasional diamond in the rough from Burundi
and Bulgaria back then. But his biggest discovery came off-
screen. While meandering through the streets of Montreal, he
took an excursion along the city's fabled St. Lawrence Boulevard, or the Main, as he learned the natives called the street. It
was about eleven at night and he noticed something a little
unusual. There was a line-up snaking nearly around the block.
Peary figured folks were queuing up for some funky music club.
Hardly. They were patiently standing in line to get into a *deli*?
And a fairly nondescript looking one at that. He was intrigued,
all the more so since it was a stinking hot August day in
Montreal, the sort of day one would assume people would be
lining up for banana splits at a Dairy Queen, not banana peppers
at a deli. No matter. Peary waited his turn in line for nearly half
an hour, and just prior to midnight he finally figured out what
all the fuss was about. He had just undergone a religious
experience of sorts. He had devoured a Schwartz's smoked-meat
sandwich for the first time, and he could swear he was touching
base with the deities, deli-division. He was now a convert to
the cause.

So in addition to extolling the virtues of movie gems from
Burundi and Bulgaria, in his capacity as film critic for the *Boston*

Phoenix, Peary also waxed on about the joys of this tantalizing spiced beef, smoked meat, for the foodie bible *Gourmet* magazine. "Schwartz's is the best smoked meat in Montreal, therefore in the world," Peary declared in his piece for *Gourmet*. So taken was management at Schwartz's at the time that they used only this quote in their infrequent newspaper advertisements.

Peary's review is said to have sparked pilgrimages from far and wide on the planet to Schwartz's to sample this smoked meat. For his part, Peary managed never to miss attending the Montreal World Film Festival. Sure, he still enjoyed scoping the occasional tractor flick from Bulgaria or costume drama from Burundi. But the truth of the matter was that he had become addicted to Schwartz's, and needed his annual summer fix of smoked meat.

And so it is for the 29th Montreal World Film Festival that Peary is back in town with his new bride, Amy. His mission is twofold: to tuck into a Schwartz's smoked-meat sandwich and to turn Amy on to this delicacy for the first time. The latter could be problematic. Amy is a vegetarian. Peary feels a tad guilty, but not so much that he'll cease with his mission.

Amy hasn't touched meat in eight years. "I won't turn back, I tell you," she announces at our table. Schwartz's owner, Hy Diamond, sitting with us, has his doubts. He's seen vegetarians leap off the wagon before.

Peary, for his part, wastes no time digging into a plate of smoked meat, just presented to him. "Wherever else I have tried to eat smoked meat, it has been an utter failure," he confesses. "It's just so moist and tender here. It melts in your mouth. I feel like some fool talking about the joys of Betty Crocker brownies or something."

"But seriously, anything that can turn French's mustard into an elixir has to be something close to magical," Peary marvels.

Change happens slowly at Schwartz's, however, a new ceiling was
installed in the fall of 2005.

"The fatter the smoked meat, the better. I know that flies in the face of common sense. But it's all about moisture. I know that sounds like a cliché, but that's the secret to great smoked meat. That's the reason pastrami doesn't come close. That's the reason smoked meat in Toronto and Vancouver don't come close."

Diamond is nearly glowing with these words. Peary then asks Diamond for the recipe. Diamond gracefully declines. Peary picks up a steak knife, points it in Diamond's directions and asks again for the recipe. Diamond says Peary can stab him if he likes, but he still ain't spilling the spice on the recipe.

"All I'll say is that the whole world is changing, except for Schwartz's," Diamond tells Peary.

Meanwhile as this mock confrontation unfolds, Amy quietly slips a fork on to the plate of smoked meat, picks up a slice, smells it carefully, then swallows it. She licks her lips and repeats the process again. Peary and Diamond stop their jousting and break out into huge smiles. They have converted another vegetarian into a carnivore. "It's only temporary," Amy protests.

"Whatever," Peary responds.

As Amy continues to savour this once forbidden treasure, Peary bolts up from the table and bellows: "I've got it. I've finally figured it all out. It's taken nearly twenty years, but I've finally uncovered one of life's greatest mysteries."

OK, wise man, shoot:

"Smoked meat is like sex," Peary exclaims. "You don't want to eat it dry."

Peary is pleased with himself. Diamond is dumbfounded.

"Feel free to use that quote in your advertisements now," Peary implores him.

Diamond politely tells Peary he'll take it under advisement, but doesn't feel his clientele would cotton to this kinky analogy.

"Cheque, please!" Diamond then blurts. "Wait. I'm the boss!"

Epilogue

STOP THE PRESSES: Schwartz's makes the society pages for the first time in its seventy-year history. And it has nothing to do with its smoked meat.

Founder Reuben Schwartz might have plotzed at such a charitable proposition; but current owner Hy Diamond spearheaded a fundraiser for the Montreal Ovarian Cancer Initiative which represented an all-too-rare franco-anglo medical collaboration in the city between one research group from the Université de Montréal led by Dr. Diane Provencher of the Centre Hospitalier's Institut de Cancer and another research group from McGill University led by Dr. Walter Gotlieb of the Jewish General Hospital. Society bigwigs and lesser wigs, along with a deli-loving host of doctors, scientists, politicos, athletes and celebs, gathered all day and evening on September 15, 2005 at Schwartz's for the event. Luminaries like rocker Colin James and Montreal Canadiens hockey great Jean Béliveau and former Quebec justice minister Jerôme Choquette and cosmetics magnate Lise Watier noshed on smoked meat, and even spek, for lunch and dinner, even breakfast, in aid of the cause. The then-popular Montreal CHOM-FM morning-radio team of Terry DiMonte and Ted Bird broadcast their show live from Schwartz's—another first.

Diamond, whose wife succumbed to ovarian cancer, figured that he was one of the few entrepreneurs in the city who could reach out to all charitable Montrealers to support such a fundraiser. He was correct. He not only donated all proceeds of Schwartz's sales for the day to the cause, but he also prevailed upon his suppliers—both francos and anglos—to add more to the till. Close to $150,000 was collected in the battle against the "silent killer," ovarian cancer.

Oh, yeah. And fret not for Paul Martin, whose ruling Liberal Party went down to defeat in the federal election of January 23, 2006. Martin, who stepped down as Liberal leader following the election, is not without options. Sure, he could retire to his hobby farm in the bucolic Eastern Townships and watch goats graze. Or he could put to practice a lesson taught him by Schwartz's manager Frank Silva. Yes, under the Access to Information Act or a reasonable facsimile, it has been learned that Silva instructed the former Prime Minister on the fine art of hand-cutting smoked-meat. Schwartz's catered a media party for 150 at the Prime Minister's official residence in Ottawa during the summer of 2005. To help handle the stampede of hungry media hordes, Martin was given a quick cutting lesson and was then conscripted into duty.

"I've got to say he had a pretty decent cutting technique for a novice," Silva enthused after the event. "He also handled the pressure really well. I was impressed. I don't mean to be presumptuous, but if he ever needs a job, we could take him on the road for catering jobs."

Could be worse. Besides, Martin, a frequent Schwartz's visitor, would get to *fress* regularly on one of his favourite foods—and his South Beach diet be damned!

As for Stephen Harper, the Conservative leader who replaced Martin as P.M., he has yet to be spotted dropping into Schwartz's. But if Harper intends to ingratiate himself to Montrealers and, eventually, to get a Conservative elected in the city, he'd better follow the lead of former P.M.s Pierre Trudeau, Brian Mulroney, Jean Chrétien and Martin, and go for a shvitz-cum-smoked-meat sandwich. And for the love of Alberta beef, Steve, please don't be ordering your smoked meat on white with mayo. It will come back to haunt you.

In the ensuing years, following the first and second printings of this book, both Armande Toupin Chartrand and Morris "The Shadow" Sherman passed away. But Schwartz's "custodian" Hy Diamond has remained true to his pledge about refusing to franchise—despite still being inundated with offers to set up operations everywhere from Alaska to, yes, Zaire.

On the other hand, Diamond had made a few small concessions to modern times: he finally replaced his eighty-year-old charcoal grill with a newer model and he opened up a take-out smoked-meat spot adjacent to the eatery—but on weekends only—to accommodate the throngs lined up on the street. According to lore, it was either that or get charged with assembling a non-authorized demonstration. The politics of deli can, after all, get dirty, too.

Illustration Credits

Frontispiece, Simon Dardick; 19 courtesy of Hy Diamond; 23, 24, 29, 34 (bottom), 39, 40 Simon Dardick; 48 courtesy of Hy Diamond; 51, 53, 57 Simon Dardick; 61 courtesy Hy Diamond; 65 Jennifer Weiskopf; 66, 69, 71, 73, 78, 86, 89, 90, 99 Simon Dardick; 104 courtesy Hy Diamond; 107, 108, 113, 114, 117-120, 122 courtesy Jack Lieber; 111 *Montreal Gazette*; 124, 127-28 courtesy Jack Lieber; 108, 124 NFB; 127 courtesy Jack Lieber; 142, 146 Simon Dardick.

Index

Montreal *Star* 80, 106, 108-109
Moonglow Romance 112
Morris, William *see* Lord Nuffield
Mulroney, Brian 88, 134
Myers, Mike 46

National Film Board of Canada 49-50, 109
National Geographic 20
National Hockey League 74
Nelli, Mike 67-68, 71
New York Times, The 20
Newman, Rick 43-45, 47
Ngom, Ahmadou Fadilou 35
Nuffield, Lord 112

Office de la langue Française (OLF) 37-38, 41
O'Hara, Catherine 46
Old Brewery Mission 49
Onassis, Jacqueline Kennedy 115
Orr, Bobby 75
Orsato, Brian 78

Palace Theatre 105
Pastrami 16-18, 43, 47, 62
Peary, Gerald 129-130, 132
Pentelis, Peter 87-88, 91
Phillips, Mark 80
Phizicky, Stephen 79-81
Pickman, Deb 33
Pinaheiro, Manny 68-70
Pope John XXIII 115-116
Provencher, Dr. Diane 133

Quebec Aces 73
Quebec Senior Hockey League 73
Queen Elizabeth II 115
Queue de Cheval 91
Quick, Moira 33

Rayner, Michael 33
Richard, Maurice 75
Richards, Keith 27
Richler, Mordecai 81
Rivers, Joan 64, 67
Robinson, Danny 44, 48
Rosalie's 91
Rudman, Itzak 15-16
Ryan 50

Sawiries, Mike 103
Saykaly, Mark "Marky" 53-57
Schwartz, Reuben 13, 16, 18-19, 21, 53, 68, 86, 88, 94-95, 98, 100-104, 106, 121, 126, 128, 133
Scions of Hydra, The 33
Second Avenue deli 43, 47
Seeing Things 58
Shadow, The *see* Morris Sherman
Sherman, Morris "The Shadow" 95-98, 100-104, 135
Silva, Frank 21-22, 25, 27, 35, 83, 85-86, 134
Silverman, Jerry 62-64
Smoked Meat Pete 19
Snowdon deli 18, 93
Sokach, Muriel 82
Sokach, Peter 82
Spare Change 50
St. Cyr, Lili 11
St. Joseph's Oratory 13
Stage deli 18, 43
Stanley Cup 72, 75
Strauss, Kalman 29

Taylor, Bruce 80
Tierney, Kevin 52, 67
Toronto Maple Leafs 78